NORTH CAROLINA
STATE BOARD OF COMMUNITY COLLEGES
LIBRARIES
SAMPSON TECHNICAL COLLEGE

C0-DNI-832

Legal Almanac Series No. 4

REAL ESTATE LAW FOR HOMEOWNER AND BROKER

by Parnell J.T. Callahan
& Louis M. Nussbaum

*This Legal Almanac has been revised
by the Oceana Editorial Staff*

Irving J. Sloan
General Editor

**Oceana Publications, Inc.
Dobbs Ferry, New York 10522**

Library of Congress Cataloging in Publication Data

Callahan, Parnell Joseph Terence.
    Real estate law for homeowner and broker.

    (Legal almanac series; no. 4)
    Includes index.
    1. Vendors and purchasers--United States--Popular works. 2. Real property--United States--Popular works.
I. Nussbaum, Louis M., joint author.   II. Title.
KF665.Z9C33   346.73'043   79-28178
ISBN 0-379-11121-7

©Copyright 1980 by Oceana Publications, Inc.

All rights reserved. No part of this publication may be reproduced or transmitted in any form or by any means, electronic or mechanical, including photocopy, recording, xerography, or any information storage and retrieval system, without permission in writing from the publisher.

Manufactured in the United States of America.

TABLE OF CONTENTS

Preface iv

Chapter 1
REAL ESTATE AND PROPERTY RIGHTS —
   SOME BASIC PRINCIPLES 1

Chapter 2
THE DEED — CONVEYING OWNERSHIP 17

Chapter 3
CONTRACTING FOR PURCHASING AND
   BUYING REAL ESTATE 43

Chapter 4
CLOSING TITLE 69

Chapter 5
POINTERS FOR BROKERS 81

Chapter 6
THE LANDLORD AND TENANT
   RELATIONSHIP 95

Chapter 7
INSURING THE HOME 104

Glossary 112

Index 119

Series Conversion Table 121

PREFACE

Home ownership is an unusual and rare investment in one's lifetime. While a knowledge of legal principles is necessary to avoid costly errors, an understanding of economic and social factors is of equal importance to the owner.

Before a single dollar is invested or a single contract is signed, an owner should consider the following factors:

1—Proximity of transit facilities
2—Location of schools
3—Parks and Playgrounds
4—Neighborhood and neighbors
5—Parking areas
6—Shopping convenience
7—House of Worship locations
8—Adequate local utilities, e.eg., gas, electric, telephone
9—Health conditions; sewage disposal, refuse removal
10—Construction of a home; drainage; type of land, e. g., refilled land

The home owner should avail himself of professional advice. In advance of buying or building, consultation with an architect, real estate broker, an appraiser and an attorney, will be of incalculable value.

Chapter 1
REAL ESTATE AND PROPERTY RIGHTS — SOME BASIC PRINCIPLES

The object of this book is to state in plain words the law governing the buying of a home; the subsequent peaceful enjoyment of its possession, and then its sale, either through the direct efforts of the owner or employment of a real estate broker as a medium.

Its further purpose is to set forth the rights, privileges and duties of the home owner as they are recognized by law and enforced in our courts.

It is a natural assumption of ownership, that when an individual receives a deed to real property, that he owns it absolutely. However, such ownership is subject to various curbs and restrictions created by law, in order to control the property use for the promotion of the health and welfare of adjoining community home owners.

The following are examples of governmental restrictions:

Governmental Limitations

       1—Exercise of Police Power
       2—Eminent Domain
       3—Taxation Powers

EXERCISE OF POLICE POWER: The State as a sovereign power, on its own initiative or by delegation to local governing units can curtail the full use of real estate by the adoption of zoning regulations, building, fire and health regulations.

ZONING: The fundamental purpose of the zoning power is to prevent overcrowding of land; avoid undue population concentration; provide adequate light, air and sunshine to building occupants; facilitate traffic and lessen street congestion; and the conservation of property values.

Laws accomplishing these ends are a valid police power.

EMINENT DOMAIN: The government has the right to condemn or take your property, if needed for a public use, on payment of a fair price. Examples of public uses:

  1—Public buildings; a court house
  2—Creation of parkways, streets, roads
  3—Increased transit facilities
  4—Public health structures; Hospitals
  5—Parking fields, Public markets
  6—Slum Clearance and elimination of substandard areas.

The right to fair and just compensation to the property owner is guaranteed and protected by the United States Constitution under the clause that "no person shall be deprived of his life, liberty or "property", except by due process and payment of just compensation.

The value of the property taken is fixed by appraisers, appointed by the courts, and it must be the fair market value of the property, as of the date of the government taking.

A definition of "Fair Market Value" as stated in a leading case, sets forth the following rule in determining the damage award:

"Fair Market Value" means neither panic value; auction value; speculative value; nor a value fixed by depressed or inflated prices. The mere absence of competitive buyers does not establish a lack of a real market. However, a true market may be established only where there are willing buyers and sellers in substantial numbers. When there is no real market, as of the time of condemnation, proof of such loss occasioned because of the public use appropriation by the government, may be shown by evidence of the "fair market value, at the nearest earlier date when there was a fair market, provided the property is substantially in the same condition as at that prior time.

TAXATION POWERS: Taxes are charges imposed on property to raise money for public needs, and every owner of property holds title subject to the government power to tax, and is charged with notice, that periodically a tax will be levied upon his land. Ownership of property, particularly in large cities, should be promptly recorded and filed also with the local unit charged with the collection of taxes. At the present time, a failure to pay a tax due, no matter how small, without further billing, and at the expiration of the local statutory grace period, will cause the public sale of the land.

As distinguished from taxes, assessments do not occur regularly. An assessment may cover the entire cost of a local improvement, or only a portion of this cost, in which latter case, the remainder is paid from general taxes. Until paid, an assessment is a lien against the owner's property. In the purchase of real estate, affected by an assessment, payable in annual installments, as each of these installments fall due, they become liens on the property. The unpaid assessments, which become due thereafter, subsequent to the transfer of title, would have to be discharged by the purchaser, without liability on the part of the seller. For example, in New York City, certain assessments may, at the option of the owner, be divided into ten installments. In the absence of a clause in the contract, requiring the seller to pay and discharge the entire assessment imposed, a buyer would, in effect, be paying twice for the improvements to the property.

Private Limitations of Ownership

Although ownership of property gives the right to its use absolutely, except for the creation of nuisance, there are, in addition to the limitations imposed by law, for example, right of condemnation, zoning regulations, and taxing powers, certain other limitations may be created by restrictions in the deed of ownership from the seller. An owner of a plot of land, may subdivide this property, sell each of these lots individually, and by means of restrictive clauses placed in these deeds, for the purpose of benefiting the owners of the adjoining lots provide, that buildings may be constructed only of a specific type; below a certain height, or set back a definite distance from the front boundary. Such limitations bind future owners of the property, and for a violation of such restriction, any owner or subsequent owner may sue to restrain such acts.

A. REAL ESTATE

When you buy "REAL ESTATE" or "REAL PROPERTY", just what do you expect to acquire? What is the extent of your ownership? How much of what is on the land belongs to you, and how much may the seller keep for himself? When you sell "REAL ESTATE," just how much do you want to sell, and what do you want to keep?

Suppose there are some sturdy old oak trees, and a neat pile of oak logs, freshly cut down just a week before the delivery of the deed made you the owner of the land. And suppose that in that old colonial house, of which you are now the owner, there are some beautiful old wall fixtures and some hand carved wall panels which slide out very nicely for cleaning. Who owns them after the property is sold

The growing trees are REAL PROPERTY to the same extent as the land on which they are growing. The logs, having been severed from the REAL PROPERTY, are personal property, and do not pass with the land. Inside the house, an almost identical situation prevails. The wall fixtures, being affixed permanently to the house are REAL PROPERTY, but the hand carved panels which can be removed without damage to the house, and without changing their nature or structure, are personal property, and do not pass with the building unless the contract of sale specifically provides for their inclusion.

Of course, there is little difficulty when we deal with land itself, which we can easily recognize as REAL PROPERTY. When we come to the growing crops, however, the law varies somewhat from state to state, and from crop to crop. Trees or timber, whose growth extends over more than one year are about universally regarded as REAL PROPERTY as long as they are affixed to the land, but as personal property, not necessarily passing with the land, once they have been severed. On the other hand, crops which mature or are harvested within a year are usually regarded as personal property.

If you are in doubt, ask your lawyer BEFORE you sign the contract for the purchase or sale of the land.

Fixtures which are built in or permanently attached to the land or house become part of it, and are considered as REAL PROPERTY; but if they can be moved without damage to themselves and the real estate, they are personal property rather than REAL PROPERTY.

While the Real Property Law of the State of New York, and of many other states defines "REAL PROPERTY" as "lands, tenements and hereditaments and chattels real, except a lease for a term not exceeding three years," the situation may be summarized by reference to the old civil law, which designated REAL PROPERTY as "immovables" and personal property as "movables."

B. WHO MAY OWN REAL PROPERTY

Any citizen of the United States may become an owner of land or real estate. No state or community has the right to infringe upon a citizen's right to inherit or purchase either real or personal property. In most states, aliens and even alien enemies are entitled to hold property although their power to transfer, sell or mortgage their property is usually subject to restriction. In other states there are some limitations placed on the class of aliens who may hold real property, and a transfer to such an alien may be absolutely void. If you are in any doubt as to whether you may hold real property in a particular state, be sure to consult your lawyer before you sign a contract of sale. By the same token, if you are about to sell your property, make proper inquiries to insure against having your property tied up under a contract of sale to a person or persons who may not legally acquire title.

While a state may not limit the right of a citizen to own property, the question of restrictive covenants is altogether different, and the United States Supreme Court has held that a restrictive covenant, or a clause in his deed prohibiting sale to, or occupancy by members of a certain race, religion, or sect, is not a violation of constitutional rights, because it is the action of an individual, and not of the state itself. However, the Supreme Court has ruled these covenants unenforcible, since their enforcement by a court—an arm of government—would be unconstitutional. Thus a seller may freely violate a racial restrictive covenant since no legal action to prevent it can be successfully brought. If, however, the seller is content to be bound by the covenant, the prospective purchaser is powerless to force action. If you feel that there is any doubt as to the validity of a transfer, before you attempt to make a purchase or sale, check with your lawyer.

The fact that you are an infant (and any person under legal age is an infant even if he is six foot tall, weighs two hundred pounds and is a Lieutenant Colonel in the Air Forces) will not bar you from holding REAL PROPERTY, but may cause considerable difficulty when you try to sell or transfer the property. In most states, a married woman has the same right as her husband to buy, hold, sell or mortgage real estate.

C. WAYS IN WHICH TITLE OR OWNERSHIP MAY BE ACQUIRED

(1) *Deed or Purchase*: Most people who own REAL PROPERTY today acquired their land by buying and paying for it. They agreed with the former owner upon a price and in return for the purchaser's money, the seller gave a written acknowledgment to the effect that he surrendered to the purchaser all rights to the property. This transaction is called a sale or conveyance, and the written acknowledgment is what we know as the "deed" to the REAL PROPERTY. The deed is written evidence of ownership, and as soon as it is recorded in the office of the County Clerk or the Register, it serves notice on the world of the ownership of the property. The deed will be signed by the "Grantor" or person who is relinquishing ownership, and will name the new owner, or "Grantee."

(2) *Inheritance*: After your father's funeral, his will is filed and probated, and you learn that he has willed or "left" to you the old family homestead, consisting of the farmhouse, fifty-six acres of land and two barns. The procedure is the same regardless of whether the REAL PROPERTY consists of a homestead, a farm, business property, or vacant land. You acquire the property, and become the owner, not through purchase, but by inheritance. You will not receive a deed to the property, and your title will arise

from the will. You may, if you wish, record the will in the office of the County Clerk, where it will be additional evidence of your ownership of the property and your right to transfer title, but such a recording is not necessary to give you a "clear title."

Let us suppose, on the other hand, that your father leaves no will, and that he is survived by your mother, and by your three sisters and brothers. You all become part owners on your father's death, and proceedings in the Surrogate's, Orphans' or Probate Court usually will be necessary to give you a "clear" or "marketable" title, since a prospective purchaser, in addition to wanting to know just who was entitled to a share of the property, will want to be sure that all the owners or heirs are surrendering their rights in the property. If your brother Tom returned to Australia after getting out of the Army, he must join in any deed or conveyance which the rest of the heirs may desire to make. If he fails or refuses to join, you cannot give a "clear" or "marketable" title.

(3) *Public Grant*: Th first settlers in the United States came ashore and helped themselves to vacant land. In some places, they really pushed the Indians out, while in other places, like Manhattan Island, they acquired the land from the Indians by purchase. As the settlements spread out, however, there were large areas of land owned by the Government. A large part of this land was distributed or given away by the Government. Occasionally, the new owner made a payment to the Government, which may have been the local, state or Federal Government. On other occasions he promised to make some improvements or to perform some services, such as building a dam, road or railroad, while at still other times the land was merely opened for settlement and colonization, and the first person to make his claim and record it became the owner. Under various Homestead Acts, settlers were given a conditional title, which did not become absolute until after three or five years of continuous occupancy and operation. Even today it is possible for a citizen to acquire title under the Homestead Acts. The details of the areas which are still open for settlement under these Acts, and the requirements for settlement, may be obtained from the Department of Interior, Washington, D. C.

(4) *Adverse Possession*: Suppose that you buy a parcel of property, and build a house and garage. Six months after you have finished the house, the owner of the adjoining lot calls on you one day

and tells you that you made a mistake and that the east side of your house is seven feet over the line on his property. You bring out a survey which shows that you own the seven feet and one more foot. Your neighbor says it is wrong, and you say it is right.

After telling you to get your house off his land, the adjoining land-owner writes you a severe letter, ordering you to remove your house. You file the letter away with your deed and still do nothing about it except to answer his letter and tell him that you are right. Much to your surprise, the owner of the land does nothing, and before you realize it, twenty years have rolled by. Then, one day more than twenty years after you have received the letter telling you to move your house, a lawyer calls on you and tells you that his client has just bought the land next to yours and wants you to remove your house. He shows you a survey and for the first time you realize that for more than twenty years a part of your house has been on your neighbor's property. By this time, your son John is in his second year of law school, and as the lawyer tells you what his client will do, if you don't remove your house, John interrupts to ask when the house was built. When you bring out the letter written over twenty years ago, John, who has received an "A+" in his course in real estate law, smiles happily, while the visiting lawyer, looking very unhappy, reaches for his hat, and leaves without a word. As the door slams, John tells you that by remaining in possession for twenty years, under a claim adverse to that of the actual owner, you have acquired "title by adverse possession."

While the length of time required for an occupancy by adverse possession to ripen into ownership varies from state to state, the elements of (1) *possession* (your house was there and you were in it), (2) *a claim of title* (your claim that your survey was right), (3) *hostile to the other party* (he claimed that you had no right at all to be there) are all that are required. Where your neighbor made his mistake was in not acting promptly. You sometimes wondered why the neighbor on the other side, part of whose property you used as a driveway, asked you to sign a paper acknowledging that you used the driveway with his permission. He merely filed your signature with his deed, and kept his title clear.

On the other hand, if your neighbor on whose land your building encroached, had acted within a year or two after you had exchanged letters, you would have had no defense and he could have compelled you to remove your house, or to pay him a proportionate part of the value of his land. His difficulty was that he waited too long before taking action, and he actually let you become an owner by *adverse possession*. As a rule, adverse possession from ten to twenty years is required before the occupant of the land actually becomes the owner, but there is some variance from State to State.

(5) *Foreclosure*: Suppose your neighbor, Farmer Jones, finds that he needs three thousand dollars. He owns his small farm, so he hitches up the buggy, drives to the village, and calls on Mr. Gotrocks, the banker. Mr. Gotrocks lends him the money and takes a mortgage on the farm. What actually happens is that Farmer Jones agrees to pay back the three thousand dollars and pledges his farm as security. The transaction is almost the same as if he were to pawn his watch or his automobile, but here, he actually retains possession of the pawned or pledged property, in this case, his farm. After the mortgage is drawn up and signed, it is "filed" or recorded at the office of the County Clerk, and anyone attempting to buy the farm will be required to purchase it subject to the outstanding mortgage. Farmer Jones owns the "fee" or legal title, but the "equitable" title belongs to Mr. Gotrocks, the mortgagee. Farmer Jones, having given the mortgage, is the mortgagor. He has the right to clear his title by "redeeming" the land and paying the mortgage. Suppose, however, that after a few years, instead of finding himself in a position where he can pay back the money, he is absolutely penniless. He has been offered a job in the City and has decided to abandon his farm. One fine morning, he disappears, and Mr. Gotrocks owns the mortgage but not the farm. If Mr. Gotrocks merely walks in and takes possession of the farm, he does so subject to Farmer Jones' right of redemption. In other words, Farmer Jones may return, say to Mr. Gotrocks "Here is your three thousand land interest. Give me back my farm," and Mr. Gotrocks would be required by law to comply. In order to "foreclose" the right of redemption and to acquire legal title to the farm, Mr. Gotrocks must go through a foreclosure proceeding. He first calls on his lawyer, who prepares a complaint and a "lis pendens." The lis pendens is filed with the Clerk of the Court and in the Office of the County

Clerk, and is notice to all the world that a foreclosure suit has been begun. If Farmer Jones, far away in the City, attempts to sell his farm, he will sell it subject not only to the mortgage, but also to the pending foreclosure action. If Farmer Jones can be found within the State, he must be served personally with the summons and complaint in the foreclosure action. If he cannot be found, it will be necessary for Mr. Gotrocks to publish the summons and notice of foreclosure. After the publication has been completed, or after the summons and complaint have been served personally on Farmer Jones, he will have twenty or thirty days within which to file an answer. He may claim that he actually paid the mortgage, that it was usurious, or that it was obtained under duress, or he may not even bother to answer. After his failure to answer or after a trial, a judgment of foreclosure will be entered and the Sheriff or a Referee appointed by the Court will sell the property at auction. As a rule, the mortgagee "buys in" the property for the amount of the mortgage and no money changes hands. However, if the property is worth considerably more than the mortgage, there may be competition among various buyers and enough money may be realized to satisfy the mortgage and to leave something for the mortgagor, in our case, Farmer Jones. It will take Mr. Gotrocks anywhere from one week to two years to complete his foreclosure, and it will cost him anywhere from ten dollars to three hundred and fifty dollars, exclusive of what he will have to pay his lawyer. You may be in a position to acquire property by taking over a mortgage and foreclosing. You may also be in a position where the mortgagor, rather than put you to the expense of a foreclosure, will give you a deed. By following this procedure, you will be on somewhat shaky ground, since other creditors may claim that the transfer to you was an unlawful preference, giving you a priority over them in collecting the debts owed by the mortgagor.

On the other hand, suppose that you, yourself, are unable to pay your mortgage. If the mortgage is a small one, it may be better for you to sell your property subject to the mortgage and to realize enough from the sale to pay the mortgagee. If the mortgagee is anxious to obtain your property, you may be able to work out a more satisfactory bargain by saving him from the delay, bother and expense of foreclosure. Every person who has an interest in the property must be served with papers or notified, actually or by publication, of the existence of the foreclosure action. Even tenants must be notified, or the new owner will not be able to evict them under the judgment of foreclosure. Foreclosures are technical legal proceedings. You should no more attempt a foreclosure without a lawyer than you should attempt an appendectomy without a doctor.

(6) *Accretion*: Suppose you own a lovely house right on the beach. You have been somewhat worried about possibility of the bay washing away your land, so before going back home for the winter, you erect a small bulkhead. To your great surprise, when you arrive the following summer, you find that the bay has built up, around your bulkhead, an additional one hundred feet of land. Although this land was not acquired by purchase, inheritance, foreclosure, public grant, or adverse possession, it nevertheless belongs to you. Accretion is the increase of REAL ESTATE by the addition of portions of soil by gradual deposit through the operation of natural causes. If you own land on the bank of a river and the unfortunate land owner up stream suffers the loss of part of his land, the fact that his land is deposited on your land, thus doubling the size of your property, does not give him any rights against you. You must own land in order to acquire land by accretion, but any deposits on your own land adding to its dimensions belong to you.

D. ESTATES OR DEGREES OF POSSESSION OF REAL PROPERTY

(1) *Fee Simple*: Your deed will usually include the words "To John Purchaser, his heirs and assigns forever." This conveys to you a "Fee Simple" the highest type of ownership of REAL PROPERTY. A Fee Simple gives you absolute ownership and permits you to sell, mortgage, convey and devise your land by Will. It excludes all qualifications or restrictions as to the persons to whom you may transfer it, and it is yours as long as you live, if you do not sell it, give it away, or mortgage it and then fail to pay the mortgage. In some states, the word "heirs" must be included, while in other states the words "and assigns" by itself is sufficient. To safeguard against all changes or idiosyncracies, it is always well to have the deed include the words "To John Purchaser, his heirs and assigns forever." In this way there never can

be any question that John Purchaser is the absolute owner and that there are no limitations, restrictions or qualifications placed on his ownership of the property.

(2) *Life Estate*: An estate for life is an ownership of property, absolute but held by the tenant for his own life or for the life or lives of one more person. When the measure of the duration of the estate is the tenant's own life, it is simply called an "estate for life." On the other hand, when the measure of the duration is the life of some other person, it is called an "estate per autre vie" or "estate for a life of another."

A life estate may be created either by an act of the parties, or by operation of law. In states where the wife's right of dower or the husband's right of curtesy still exists, a life estate may be created by operation of law. On the death of the husband, the wife may have a life estate in all or in part of the REAL PROPERTY owned by the husband, not only at the time of his death, but also on property owned by him at any time during the marriage. Once a life estate is created by operation of law, only the life tenant may do something to terminate or defeat the estate.

If you are buying REAL PROPERTY from a married man or a married woman, if you want to be sure that you do not find yourself holding title subject to a life estate, insist that the wife or husband join in the deed. Do this even in states where there is no right to dower or curtesy, since your purpose is not to win a law suit involving your title, but to avoid a law suit. On the other hand, you yourself may desire to create a life estate. You may want your wife to live in your house after your death, but not wishing to offend any one of your four children, you may not want to give the house to anyone individually. You, therefore, provide in your will that your wife is to have a life estate in your house, and that upon her death, the life estate is to terminate and the title to your house is to pass to your four children equally. As long as your wife owns the life estate, she may harvest the crops and exercise all incidents of ownership which do not affect the permanent character of the property. She may repair the property, but unless the persons who will be the owners after the termination of her life estate, give their permission, she may not tear it down and may not make alterations which will change its nature to any substantial degree, such as changing it from a residence to a store.

The persons who will become owners after the termination of the life estate are called "remaindermen."

(3) *Estate for Years*: An estate for years is an interest in lands which exists solely by virtue of a contract for the possession of lands for a definite and limited period of time. It may range from a period of one or two years to nine hundred and ninety-nine years or more, and the extent of ownership will be determined both by the lease and by the intention of the parties.

(4) *Future Estates*: An estate or possession which is to commence in the future is known as a "Future Interest" or "Future Estate." It includes (1) *remainders*, the remnants of an estate in land or REAL PROPERTY which depend upon the termination of a particular prior estate; (2) *reversions*, the residue of estates which remains in the Grantor and which is to return to him after the determination of some particular estate granted by him after the grant is completed; and (3) *estates limited to commence in possession at some future day*, either with or without the intervention of a prior estate, or the termination of a period of time. They may be created by the voluntary act of the parties, or by operation of law in the same manner as life estates.

(5) *Leaseholds*: A leasehold is an "estate" or "possession" of REAL PROPERTY held by virtue of a lease. It may be an estate for years or an estate for an indefinite period, such as a lease for the time while a certain ferry or railroad is in operation. If the period of the leasehold is for more than one year, the lease must be in writing to be valid. An oral lease is permitted for any period less than one year.

(6) *Joint Ownership*: When you and your wife buy a house, the deed will probably be drawn to "John Purchaser and Jane Purchaser, His Wife." On the other hand, when you and brother Bill decide to buy some property, and he does not have the money at the same time that you do, you may buy your interest in the property, and three months later, the seller, receiving his money from Bill may give him a separate deed for his interest. A little later on, you and your brother, Tom, decide to buy a lot in town, where you plan to erect a grocery store. You pool your money, and

one deed is delivered to "John Purchaser and Thomas Purchaser jointly."

Three different types of joint ownership have thus been entered. You and your brother Bill are *"tenants in common"* and you are a party to a *"tenancy in common."* You have joint possession, but you have separate and distinct titles. You might own one-fourth and Bill three-fourths, or you may own equal shares. When you die, Bill will have no interest in your share of the property, but it will pass to your heirs regardless of Bill's wishes.

On the other hand, the property which you have bought in town and on which you plan to build your grocery store is held by you and Tom as *joint tenants,* and you are a party to a *"joint tenancy."* The four elements of joint tenancy are (1) *unity of time of acquisition,* (2) *unity of interest,* (3) *unity of title,* and (4) *unity of possession.* To be joint tenants, you must have the interest in the property; you must have acquired it by the same conveyance, and hold it jointly and by the same undivided possession. Joint tenancy, like tenancy by the entirety, carries with it the right to survivorship. When Tom dies, his interest in the jointly owned property will not be transmitted to his heirs, but instead will pass directly to you. Likewise, if you should predecease him, you will have nothing to say about your interest in the property, and it will beyong to Tom by virtue of his right of survivorship.

The third type of joint ownership is the *"tenancy by the entirety,"* by which you and your wife will own your house when it is deeded to you as "John Purchaser and Jane Purchaser, his wife." Be careful just how the deed is drawn. You may not want a joint tenancy, and unless the deed recites "John Purchaser and William Purchaser, as Tenants in Common," you may find yourself in difficulty. As a rule, unless the deed contains the words, "as joint tenants," or "jointly" you will become tenants in common. but to be safe, it is best to include the words "as tenants in common."

When you and your wife take a deed to the property, the mere statement that she is your wife is sufficient to make you *tenants by the entirety.* A tenancy by the entirety is identical with a joint tenancy, except that the joint tenants are recognized as husband and wife, and consequently are regarded as one person.

Discuss this point with your lawyer, since it may be difficult to change the type of ownership once the deed is delivered, and years later, it may not only be impossible, but may result in an inequitable or unpleasant situation.

E. THE COUNTY CLERK AND THE REGISTER

When you buy a suit of clothes or a watch, you pay your money and take your newly acquired property. Of course, you cannot do this with REAL PROPERTY. How then are you to be protected? What is there to stop William Seller from having given one deed last week, delivering another to you tomorrow morning, and a third to someone else next week? How can you protect yourself?

Once a deed has been executed and acknowledged, it should be recorded *immediately* in the Office of the County Clerk or the Register. If it is not recorded, and next week William Seller executes a deed to someone else, and that deed *is* recorded, you will find yourself completely out in the cold, with a worthless piece of paper, and no land. All states of the union maintain offices where deeds may be recorded. If your conveyance, whether it is a deed or a mortgage, is not recorded, no one is put on notice that you are the new owner, or mortgagee, and a subsequent purchaser who records his deed before you record yours will own the property, while you will be excluded completely. You may wonder why your lawyer, as soon as the title is closed, walks across the street to the Courthouse and steps down stairs to the office of the County Clerk, where he pays a recording fee and deposits the deed. He has not wasted any time, but has insured you against the possibility of another deed being recorded. Lawyers sometimes schedule title closings for Saturday afternoon, since they can then check the deeds recorded at the Office of the County Clerk at closing time on Saturday morning, and then appear at the County Clerk's Office, when it opens on Monday, to record the new deed. The County Clerk maintains large books called "Libers" in which he records deeds and mortgages. A full copy of the deed is recorded. In most states, it is copied, but in a great many communities photostatic copies are made and filed. The original deed is then returned to you. The

15

recorded copies of the deeds are open to the inspection of anyone who may be interested.

Chapter 2

THE DEED — CONVEYING OWNERSHIP

Every interest in real property, except a lease for period of less than one year, must be evidenced by a writing or "conveyance." This writing, if it conveys and transfers the ownership of the property, is called a deed, and a deed, in turn, has been defined as "a written instrument, containing a contract or agreement, which has been delivered and accepted by obligee or covenantee". The deed is a written statement to the effect that the grantor or seller transfers certain rights in the real property to the grantee or purchaser. It is not signed by the grantee. It must not only be in writing, signed by the grantor, but in order to be recorded, it must be "acknowledged" as well. The grantor or person executing the deed must appear before a competent officer of court, and declare that it is in effect his act or deed. After his identity is made known to the officer or the court, the signature of the officer and his seal, or the seal of the court will be affixed. The deed may then be recorded, and it may be received in evidence in court without any further proof of authenticity or execution. If, however, the deed is to be in some county where the officer is not empowered to act, or in another state, a certificate of the County Clerk to the effect that the seal is, in fact, the seal of the court, or that the officer is empowered to administer oaths, must be affixed. The persons authorized to take acknowledgments are a judge or clerk of any court of record, a notary public or commissioner of deeds, the mayor or recorder of a city, a surrogate or special county judge, county clerk, attorney or counsellor at law exercising the powers of a notary public, justice of the peace, town councilman, village police justice, and a master or register in chancery. The person must, however, have some seal or stamp of authority and, as previously stated, if the deed is to be recorded or offered in evidence in any locality where the official is not authorized to act in his official capacity, a County Clerk's certificate or a certicate from the proper authority must be affixed. Outside the United States, authorizations may be taken before the proper officials of the local government, whose act must then be certified. It is usually safer to have the acknowledgment made by an American Consul or Vice-Consul, Ambassador, Minister, Charge d'Affairs, or Commercial Attache, since the seal of the Consulate or Embassy will then satisfy all requirements of authentication. The Uniform Acknowledgment Act, which governs execution and acknowledgment of instruments, is in effect in Arizona, Arkansas, Maryland, New Hampshire, Oregon, Pennsylvania, South Dakota, and Wisconsin, but it differs only slightly from the law in the remaining States of the Union.

Any person, except an infant, idiot, or person of unsound mind, may execute a deed. The disabilities of married women have been removed in most states, and as a rule they may execute deeds. Many states, however, do not permit either a husband or wife to deed away property without the consent and acquiescence of the other spouse.

A. EXECUTION AND ACKNOWLEDGMENT

The form of acknowledgment is as follows:

STATE OF WASHINGTON)
)ss:
COUNTY OF CLALLAM)

On the 17th day of March, 1979, before me personally appeared ROBERT EMMETT, to me known and known to me to be the person described in and who executed the within deed, and who acknowledged to me that he executed the same.

John Broker (Signed)
JOHN BROKER

NOTARY PUBLIC, COUNTY OF CLALLAM
State of Washington
King Co. No. 123

This acknowledgment will appear at the end of your deed, directly under the line on which the grantor or seller has signed his name. The seller, if not known, personally to the Notary Public, must produce some identification. At times, a notary public or judge may refuse to take a signature if he considers the identification insufficient. If the deed is to be recorded in some County other than Clallam or King or in some other State, your lawyer will take your deed to the Office of the County Clerk, who, for a fee of twenty-five cents will affix his official seal and will paste on the deed a printed certicate to the effect that JOHN BROKER is a notary public, qualified to administer oaths. If you buy your home from a corporation, the acknowledgment will be in slightly different form.

STATE OF WASHINGTON)
)ss:
COUNTY OF CLALLAM)

On the 17th day of March, in the year 1979, before me personally came ROBERT EMMETT, to me known, who, being by me duly sworn, did depose and say: That he resides in the City of Seattle, State of Washington; that he is the president of the SHAMROCK BUILDING CORPORATION, the corporation described in and which executed the above-instrument, that he knows the seal of said corporation; that the seal affixed to said instrument is such corporate seal; that it was so affixed by order of the board of directors of said corporation, and that he signed his name thereto by like order.

JOHN BROKER
John Broker (Signed)
NOTARY PUBLIC, COUNTY OF CLALLAM
State of Washington
Certificate on File Clallam Co. No. G10
King Co. No. 123

B. REVENUE STAMPS

The United States Government imposes a tax of $1.10 on each one thousand ($1,000.00) dollars which changes hands in a REAL ESTATE transaction. This tax is paid by the seller, and the Internal Revenue stamps must be supplied by him, fastened to the deed, and cancelled by him. He is required to pay this tax on the actual amount of money which changes hands, regardless of the amount recited in the deed. Quite often sellers do not wish to reveal to the public the amounts received for the property, and buyers may also prefer to have the information remain secret. Consequently, they recite in the deed, "Ten ($10.00) dollars and other good and valuable consideration," but they must nevertheless affix to the deed one dollar and ten cents ($1.10) revenue stamps for each one thousand ($1,000.00) dollars of actual consideration. If such stamps are not affixed, the County Clerk or Register may refuse to accept the deed for recording. If you are buying property, be sure that your contract provides that the seller will deliver a deed, duly executed, with cancelled Internal Revenue stamps affixed.

C. TYPES OF DEEDS

When you receive the deed to your house, it may be any of several forms. If you have no provision in your contract of purchase requiring the delivery of a particular form of deed, you will be compelled to accept a "quitclaim" deed. On the other hand, if your lawyer has a chance, he probably will insist on a "full covenant and warranty" deed. If you buy your REAL PROPERTY from a bank or an insurance company, you probably will receive a "bargain and sale" deed, while if you buy from an executor, or from a referee at a mortgage foreclosure, or from the Sheriff at a sale under an execution, you will receive the particular form of deed prescribed for an executor, referee or Sheriff.

(1) *Full Covenant and Warranty Deed*: The form of this deed is as follows (The deed is usually printed; the words which have been inserted are in italics):

1. This indenture, made the *seventeenth* day of March nineteen
2. hundred and *seventy-nine* between *William Vendor*, residing at
3. *34 Victor Avenue, Hempstead, New York*, party of the first
4. part, and *Joseph A. McKinley, Jr., residing at 56 North Fre-*
5. *mont Street, Tucson, Arizona*, party of the second part,
6. Witnesseth, that the party of the first part, in consideration of
7. *Twenty-five thousand* ($25,000) dollars, lawful money
8. of the United States, paid by the party of the second part, does
9. hereby grant and release unto the party of the second part *his*
10. *heirs* and assigns forever, ALL *that lot, piece and parcel of*
11. *land, together with the buildings and appurtenances situate*
12. *thereon, located and being in the village and town of Hemp-*
13. *stead, County of Nassau, State of New York*, and more particularly bounded and described as follows:
14.
15. *Beginning on the northerly side of Victor Avenue, at a*
17. *point one hundred sixty* (160) *feet west of the intersection of*
18. *Victor Avenue and Broadway, and running due north one*
19. *hundred* (100) *feet, thence west fifty* (50) *feet long a line*
20. *parallel to the northerly side of Victor Avenue, thence south*
21. *one hundred one* (101) *feet to the northerly side of Victor*
22. *Avenue, thence easterly along the northerly side of Victor*
23. *Avenue fifty feet to the point or place of beginning*, together
24. with the appurtenances and all the estate and rights of the
25. party of the first part in and to said premises.
26. To have and to hold the premises herein granted unto the
27. party of the second part *his heirs* and assigns forever. And
28. said *William Vendor* covenants as follows:
29. FIRST. That said *William Vendor* is seized of said premises
30. in fee simple, and has good right to convey the same;
31. SECOND. That the party of the second part shall quietly en-
32. joy the premises;
33. THIRD. That the said premises are free from incumbrances;

21

34. FOURTH. That the party of the first part will execute or pro-
35. cure any further necessary assurance of the title to said prem-
36. ises;
37. FIFTH. That said *William Vendor* will forever warrant the
38. title to said premises.
39. In witness whereof, the party of the first part has hereunto
40. set his hand and seal the day and year first above written.
41. In presence of: *William Vendor* (*Signed*)
42. *Thomas Broker* (Signed)

COUNTY OF SUFFOLK)
)ss:
STATE OF NEW YORK)

On the seventeenth day of March, nineteen hundred and forty-eight, before me personally appeared WILLIAM VENDOR, to me known and known to me to be the person described in and who executed the aforesaid indenture, and who acknowledged to me that he executed the same.

John Swearem (*Signed*)
JOHN SWEAREM
NOTARY PUBLIC, Residing in
New York County
New York Co. Clk's No. S32
Certificate Filed Nassau Co.
Nassau Co. Clk's No. 821
Commission Expires March 30, 1979

The word "deed" may be substituted for "indenture" in Line 1. As an added safeguard against alteration, or the claim of alteration, the date should always be written out in full, and not inserted as a number. Although lawyers now realize that it is much simpler to use the words "grantor" and "grantee" instead of the cumbersome and sometimes confusing "party of the first part" (line 3) and "party of the second part" (line 5), many of them, through force of habit, cling to outmoded legal verbiage. The residence of both parties (lines 3, 4, and 5) is required in most states if the deed is to be accepted by the recording office.

The "consideration," or the price paid (line 7) need not be recited in detail. Instead of writing out the full price of twenty-five thousand ($25,000) dollars, the parties could have written "Ten ($10.00) dollars lawful money of the United States, and other good and valuable consideration." However, in view of the requirement that Internal Revenue Stamps be affixed, no useful purpose would be served, since anyone interested could easily ascertain the purchase price by examining the Internal Revenue Stamps on the deed.

The words "his heirs and assigns forever" (line 27) are the words creating or transferring the "fee simple," or absolute and unqualified ownership of the REAL PROPERTY (Chapter 1-D (1) supra). The covenants distinguish the full covenant and warranty deed from other forms of deed.

The covenant of "seizin" (lines 29-30) means that the grantor, at the time of the execution and delivery of the deed, is the lawful owner of the property, entitled to convey and devise to other persons any interest in the REAL PROPERTY. In executing a deed with covenant, the grantor makes a warranty on which he may be sued. If it is determined subsequently that he did not have such title, and was not in effect "seized," he or his estate will be liable for all damages sustained by the grantee or party of the second part.

The covenant of "quiet enjoyment" (lines 31-32) is construed as meaning that the grantee, his heirs, or any persons acquiring title from him shall, at all times, peaceably and quietly hold, use, occupy, possess and enjoy every part of the premises described in the deed without any disturbance, law suit, trouble, or molestation, originating prior to the time the grantor delivered the deed. The grantor "warrants" or "guarantees" that at the time of the transaction, the title was good.

The "freedom from incumbrances" (line 33) is a warranty that the premises are free and clear and unencumbered from any form of gifts, deeds, mortgages, judgments, taxes, assessments, mechanic's or other liens. If title is to be taken subject to a mortgage or lien, the grantor's lawyer will add the words "except as hereinafter set forth" or except for a mechanic's lien for three hundred twenty ($320.00) dollars, filed on March 4, 1979 or whatever words may be necessary to describe adequately the incumbrance or lien.

The "further assurance" covenant (Lines 34-36) binds the grantor and his heirs to cause to be done, at the grantor's expense, every other act necessary to confirm and sustain the title of the grantee.

The fifth and last covenant, "the warranty of title" (Lines 37-38) binds the grantor to defend the title of the grantee against anyone claiming under the grantor. If the grantor die, his heirs or his estate must assume the burden, and must make good on the warranty of title.

If the grantor is a corporation rather than an individual, the recitation of the identity of the grantor (Lines 1-3) will be as follows:

"This indenture (or deed), made the seventeenth day of March, Nineteen hundred and seventy-nine, between the SHAMROCK BUILDING CO., INC., a corporation organized under the laws of the State of New York, party of the first part, having its principal office at No. 37 Wall Street, New York, New York—"

The only other discrepancy is that, in lieu of the language in lines 39 and 40, the deed will recite that:

"In Witness Whereof the party of the first part has caused its corporate seal to be hereunto affixed, and these presents to be signed by its duly authorized officer the day and year first above written."

The acknowledgment after the signature will, of course, be the corporate rather than the individual acknowledgment.

(2) *Bargain and Sale Deed*. The bargain and sale deed differs from the full covenant and warranty deed in that the grantor includes a covenant as to his own acts, but does not give any further guarantee of title. If some defect arises, the grantee himself will be responsible for its correcting. The form of the deed is as follows:

1. This indenture, made the *seventeenth* day of *March*, nine-
2. teen hundred and *seventy-nine* between SARSFIELD CORMAC
3. O'CONNELL, *residing at* 1916 *Easter Avenue, Great Neck, Nas-*
4. *sau County, State of New York, grantor, and* ARTHUR PUR-
5. CHASER, *residing at* 1921 *Victory Avenue, County of Bronx,*
6. *City and State of New York,* grantee:
6. Witnesseth, that the grantor, in consideration of *Twenty-six*
7. *thousand two hundred fifty* ($26,250.00) dollars, lawful money of
8. the United States, paid by the grantee, does hereby grant and
9. release unto the grantee *his heirs and assigns forever,* ALL
10. THAT LOT, PIECE *and parcel of land, together with the build-*

11. *ings and appurtenances situate thereon, located and being in*
12. *the village and town of Great Neck, County of Nassau, State*
13. *of New York, and more particularly bounded and described*
14. *as follows*:
15. BEGINNING *on the northerly side of Easter Avenue at a point*
16. *one hundred sixty (160) feet west of the intersection of Easter*
17. *Avenue and Broadway, and running due north one hundred*
18. *(100) feet, thence west fifty (50) feet along a line parallel to*
19. *to the northerly side of Easter Avenue, thence south one hun-*
20. *dred one (101) feet to the northerly side of Easter Avenue,*
21. *thence easterly along the northerly side of Easter Avenue fifty*
22. *(50)feet to the point or place of beginning,* together with the
23. appurtenances and all the estate and rights of the grantor in
24. and to said premises.
25. To have and to hold the premises herein granted unto the
26. Grantee, *his heirs* and assigns forever. And the grantor cove-
27. nants that he has not done or suffered anything whereby the
28. said premises have been incumbered in any way whatever.
29. In witness whereof, the grantor has hereunto set his hand
30. and seal the day and year first above written.
31.   SARSFIELD CORMAC O'CONNELL *(Signed)*
32. THOMAS BROKER *(Signed)*

STATE OF NEW YORK)
)ss:
COUNTY OF NEW YORK)

On the seventeeth day of March, nineteen hundred and forty-eight, before me personally appeared SARSFIELD CORMAC O'CONNELL, to me known and known to me to be the person described in and who executed the aforesaid indenture and who acknowledged to me that he executed the same.

        THOMAS BROKER *(Signed)*
      NOTARY PUBLIC, County of New York
         State of New York

Residing in Queens County
Queens Co. Clk's No. B 11
Bronx Co. Clk's No. 1113
Commission Expires March 30, 1979

The only covenant included in the Bargain and Sale deed is that (Lines 27-29) "the grantor has not done or suffered anything whereby said premises have been incumbered." This is included to guard against any unrecorded incumbrances or liens, and if any such incumbrance should arise, incurred by the grantor prior to the recording of the deed, but recorded subsequent to the deed, the grantor will be required to clear the title. However, any defects of title other than those resulting from the acts of the grantor will be the concern solely of the grantee.

(3) *Quitclaim Deed.* A quitclaim deed merely conveys to the grantee the entire right, title, and interest of the grantor, such as it may be. No guarantees or warranties of any sort are made. The grantor merely says, "This is all I have. It is yours," but going into no detail as to what he has, throws upon the grantee the burden of searching the title, and determining whether he desires to accept title. The form of the deed is as follows:

1. This indenture made the *seventeeth* day of *March*, nine-
2. teen hundred and *forty-eight*, between FREDERICK WEBSTER,
3. *residing at* 711 *Lucky Street, Salesburg, Illinois*, grantor, and
4. WALTER VON TONGLEN, *residing at* 66 *Boxcar Street, Brook-*
5. *lyn, New York*, grantee:
6.   Witnesseth, that the grantor, in consideration of *Twenty-seven*
7. *thousand seven hundred seventy-seven and seventy-seven one*
8. *hundredths ($27,777.77) dollars, lawful money of* the United
9. States, paid by the grantee, hereby remise, release and quit-
10. claim unto the grantee, *his heirs* and assigns forever, ALL THAT
11. LOT, PIECE *and parcel of land, together with the buildings and*
12. *appurtenances situate thereon, located and being in the village*
13. *and town of Salesburg, County of Rich, State of Illinois, and*
14. *more particularly bounded and described as follows:*
15. BEGINNING *on the northerly side of Lucky Street, at a point*
16. *one hundred fifty (150) feet west of the intersection of Lucky*
17. *Street and Broadway, and running due north one hundred*
18. *(100) feet, thence west fifty (50) feet along a line parallel to*
19. *the northerly side of Lucky Street, thence south one hundred-*
20. *One (101) feet to the northerly side of Lucky Street, thence*
21. *easterly along the northerly side of Lucky Street fifty feet (50)*

22. *to the point or place of beginning,* together with the ap-
23. purtenances and all the estate and rights of the grantor in and
24. to said premises.
25. To have and to hold the premises herein granted unto the
26. grantee, *his heirs* and assigns forever.
27. In witness whereof, the grantor has hereunto set his hand
28. and seal the day and year rst above written.
29.   FREDERICK WEBSTER (*Signed*)
30. In presence of:
31. W. E. SELLALOT (*Signed*)

STATE OF ILLINOIS)
)ss:
COUNTY OF RICH)

On the seventeenth day of March, 1979, before me personally appeared FREDERICK WEBSTER, to me known, and known to me to be the person described in and who executed the aforesaid indenture and who acknowledged to me that he executed the same.

         W. E. SELLALOT
         W. E. Sellalot

   NOTARY PUBLIC
   Residing in Rich County
   Rich County Clerk's Number I 345
   Certificate Filed Poor County
   Poor County Clerk's Number 453
   Commission expires March 30, 1979

It is not necessary for the deed to be witnessed, as long as it is acknowledged. If however, the grantor cannot appear before a notary public, it nevertheless is possible for the witness to be sworn and for the deed to be acknowledged in that way. You will note that the grantor (Line 23) conveys all *his* rights, whatever they may be. This form of deed may also be executed by either a corporation or an individual, or a group of individuals.

(4) *Executor's Deed*: Suppose your mother has left all her property to you and your three brothers and has named you as her executor. None of you want the house, since you all have your own homes, and at a family conference you decide to sell it to WILLIAM

PURCHASER. The signatures of your brothers are not necessary on the deed, although, for your own protection, it is best to have them execute consents to the sale. All that is necessary is for you to execute an executor's deed. The form of this deed will be as follows:

1. This indenture, made the *seventeenth* day of *March*, nine-
2. teen hundred and *forty-eight* between THOMAS SONANDHEIR,
3. *residing at 6722 Delafield Avenue, City and State of New*
4. *York, as executor of the last will and testament of* MARTHA
5. SONANDHEIR, *late of 6722 Delafield Avenue, City and State of*
6. *New York*, deceased, party of the first part, and WILLIAM
7. PURCHASER, *residing at 584 West 183rd Street, City and State*
8. *of New York*, party of the second part:
9. Witnesseth, that the party of the first part, by virtue of the
10. power and authority to him given in and by the said last
11. will and testament of MARTHA SONANDHEIR, *and* in considera-
12. tion of *Twenty-eight thousand* ($28,000.00) dollars, lawful money of
13. the United States, paid by the party of the second part, does
14. hereby grant and release unto the party of the second part, his
15. heirs and assigns forever, ALL THAT LOT, PIECE *and parcel of*
16. *land, together with the buildings and appurtenances situate*
17. *thereon, located and being in the village and town of New*
18. *York, County of Bronx, State of New York, and more par-*
19. *ticularly bounded and described as follows*:
20. BEGINNING *on the northerly side of Delafield Avenue, at a*
21. *point one hundred fifty* (150) *feet west of the intersection of*
22. *Delafield Avenue and Two hundred sixty-seventh Street, and*
23. *running due north one hundred* (100) *feet, thence west fifty*
24. (50) *feet along a line parallel to the northerly side of Dela-*
25. *field Avenue, thence south one hundred one* (101) *feet to the*
26. *northerly side of Delafield Avenue, thence easterly along the*
27. *northerly side of Delafield Avenue fifty* (50) *feet to the point*
28. *or place of beginning*, together with the appurtenances and
29. also all the estate which the said testatrix had at the time of
30. her decease in said premises, and also the estate therein, which
31. the party of the first part has or power to convey or dispose
32. of, whether individually or by virtue of said will or otherwise.
33. To have and to hold the premises herein granted unto the
34. party of the second part, *his heirs* and assigns forever.

35. And the party of the first part covenants that he has not
36. done or suffered anything whereby the said premises have been
37. incumbered in any way whatever.
38. In witness whereof, the party of the first part has hereunto
39. set his hand and seal the day and year first above written.
40.   THOMAS SONANDHEIR (*Signed*)
41. In presence of:
42. JOHN SWEAREM (*Signed*)

STATE OF NEW YORK)
)ss:
COUNTY OF NEW YORK)

On the *seventeenth* day of *March,* nineteen hundred and *seventy-nine,* before me personally appeared THOMAS SONANDHEIR to me known and known to me to be the person described in and who executed the aforesaid indenture and who acknowledged to me that he executed the same.

      JOHN SWEAREM (*Signed*)
      John Swearem

      NOTARY PUBLIC
      Residing in New York County
      New York County Clerk's No. S 32
      Certificate Filed Nassau County
      Nassau County Celrk's No. 821
      Commission Expires March 30, 1979

This deed is in effect a bargain and sale deed since the grantor states that he is the executor (Lines 2-4), and that as such executor he has done nothing to encumber the title (Lines 35-36). The will of MARTHA SONANDHEIR, by the time her son and executor, THOMAS, delivers the deed, will be recorded in the Surrogate's Court and may be inspected by any interested party.

(5) *Referee's Deed*: If you hold a mortgage and foreclose, or if you attend a foreclosure sale, and "buy in" the property, the Referee appointed by the Court will execute the particular form of deed prescribed for such a situation. It will be in substantially the following form:

1. This deed, made the *twenty-seventh* day of *February*, nine-
2. teen hundred and *seventy-nine* between PAUL HANGERON, re-
3. siding at 181 *Warburton Street, Yonkers, New York*, referee
5. and WILLIAM PURCHASER, *residing at* 529 *West* 113*th Street,*
6. *New York, New York*, grantee:
7. Witnesseth, that the grantor, the referee appointed in an
8. action between MARY PURCHASER *and* WILLIAM PURCHASER,
9. plaintiffs, and GEORGE MORTGAGOR *and* SALLY MORTGAGOR, de-
10. fendants, foreclosing a mortgage recorded on the *fifteenth* day
11. of *July, nineteen hundred and seventy-two*, in the office of the
12. *Clerk* of the County of *Westchester*, in liber 213 of mortgages,
13. page 127, in pursuance of a judgment entered at a Special
14. Term of the *Supreme Court of the State of New York, West-*
15. *chester County*, on the *fifth* day of February, *nineteen hun-*
16. *dred and seventy-nine* and in consideration of *Thirteen thousand*
17. ($13,000.00) dollars paid by the grantee, being the highest sum
18. bid at the sale under said judgment, does hereby grant and
19. convey unto the grantee, all *that lot, piece and parcel of land,*
20. *and the buildings and appurtenances situate thereon in the*
21. *City of Yonkers, County of Westchester*, more particularly
22. *described as follows*:
23. BEGINNING *at a point on the westerly side of Riverdale Ave-*
24. *nue at a point one hundred twenty-four* (124) *feet, south of*
25. *the intersection of Riverdale Avenue and Burns Street, and*
26. *running due west at right angles with Riverdale Avenue a*
27. *distance of seventy-five* (75) *feet, thence due south along a*
28. *line parallel to the westerly side of Riverdale Avenue forty*
29. (40) *feet, thence due east seventy-five* (75) *feet to the west-*
30. *erly side of Riverdale Avenue, thence north along the west-*
31. *erly side of Riverdale Avenue a distance of forty* (40) *feet to*
32. *the point or place of beginning.*
33. To have and to hold the premises herein granted unto the
34. grantee, his heirs and assigns forever.
35. In witness whereof, the grantor has hereunto set his hand
36. and seal.
37.   PAUL HANGERON (*Signed*)
38. In presence of:

39.   ARTHUR WITNESS (*Signed*)

COUNTY OF WESTCHESTER)
)ss:
STATE OF NEW YORK   )

On the 27th day of February nineteen *hundred and seventy-nine*, before me personally appeared PAUL HANGERON, to me known and known to me to be the person described in and who executed the foregoing instrument as the Referee duly appointed in this action by order of the Supreme Court of the State of New York, County of Westchester, entered on February fifth, nineteen hundred and seventy-nine, and who acknowledged to me that he executed the same.

ELMER BIGHAMM (*Signed*)
Elmer Bighamm
Clerk of the County of Westchester

SEAL OF
THE COUNTY OF
WESTCHESTER

Proof of the appointment of the Referee, and of his authority will be found in the Court order, which will be on file in the Office of the County Clerk. The purchaser's lawyer will inspect the order before the sale to ascertain that the Referee is qualified to act and to insure the purchaser a clear title.

E. SHOULD WE BUY?

(1) *Neighborhood Restrictions*: Let us assume that like millions of your contemporaries and many of your close friends and acquaintances, you were discharged from the Army, and finding no houses or apartments available, were forced to live with your in-laws. After several uncomfortable months you finally discovered what you and your wife considered the ideal house for your small family. Perhaps you did not find the house, but merely an ideal site consisting of a conveniently located plot of ground. Your friend, Bill Builder, assured you that he could have your house completed in four months, and you could hardly wait to sign the check.

Before you draw that check, consult your lawyer. That ideal lot or house may not be so ideal after all. If it is one vacant lot, seventy-five feet by twenty-five or thirty feet, you may find that it is too small for the kind of house the community requires. Lots in many subdivisions have been sold subject to a restriction that no house costing less than eight thousand, ten thousand, or even fifteen thousand dollars may be erected. Even if there is no such restriction in the deeds of the present and former owners, the local zoning ordinances may require you to leave seven and a half feet clearance on each side of your house, and if your lot is only twenty-five feet wide, you may have difficulty fitting your dream house into the remaining ten feet.

On the other hand, suppose that you are buying a seventy-five thousand dollar house, and in addition to no restrictions existing in the neighborhood, there are a great many twenty and twenty-five foot lots nearby. Be careful. Your seventy-five thousand dollar house of 1978, almost alone in its grandeur, may be an eight thousand dollar white elephant if, in 1988, it is surrounded by block after block of small, inelegant shacks, or rows of attached houses. Before you sign any agreement to buy land or a house, consult your lawyer. Tell him just what you plan, and just what you want. Learn something about the history of the neighborhood. Are your neighbors the kind of people with whom you will get along? Are you the friendly, gregarious fellow, or are you the more aloof, exclusive type who wants to be left alone?

See what transportation facilities are available, and whether shopping is going to be difficult. Ascertain just what you will be required to pay for gas, electric light, and water, and whether there is any danger of the rates being increased, or of the service being discontinued. Before you sign a contract, know how far children will have to travel to the nearest school, and learn as much as you can about how well the utilities and the roads bear up under winter weather conditions.

Zoning ordinances are particularly important. The six-room house may be adequate for your family as long as the family consists of your wife and two children, but then, suppose you are blessed with twins next year. Nothing daunted, you may set out to build and additional room only to learn that any addition will result in violation, since it will bring your house too close to the building line.

Let us not forget the other side of the same problem. Just what are the restrictions and regulations governing the land adjacent to that which may soon be yours? That shaded area fifty yards away is very pretty now, but would you like to see a garage built there? If you build or buy a private house, is there any danger of large apartment houses being built on the adjoining plots? Do you want to keep chickens in your back yard, or do you want to move into an area where you can be sure that no one anywhere near you will keep chickens? There will be local regulations or ordinances covering these problems, and if you consider them important, do not sign the contract until you know the answers.

On May 3, 1948, the United States Supreme Court held invalid and of no effect restrictive covenants or agreements among landowners to exclude members of a particular race or sect.

Tell your lawyer WHAT YOU WANT, and he will then make an investigation and tell you WHAT YOU MAY HAVE.

(2) *Taxes and Assessments*: "It isn't the original cost (although given the extraordinarily high prices of houses today, that original cost can also make a difference!), it's the upkeep" is just as true of a house as of an automobile. If you plan to acquire a house, you will be concerned about the expenses of maintenance. In computing your annual expenses and including allowances for repairs, fuel, and utilities, do not overlook the question of real estate taxes. Property taxes are in fact one of the greatest financial burdens carried by owners of property. While tax rates are essentially high in every part of the nation, there are still communities and cities where for a variety of reasons which are not appropriate to go into here that taxes remain significantly less. Suffice it to say, the house hunter must give careful review of the tax rates in every area he or she considers in the house search.

Another item which should not be overlooked is the possibility of special assessments. These may be levied to cover the cost of improvements such as the installation of sewers, paving of streets, or, as was encountered in New York City, the razing of an elevated railway. If the house of your dreams is in a fast growing suburb, and the sewers have not yet extended to your street, don't refuse to buy, but buy with the knowledge that in a few years, you will have your sewer and a comparatively heavy assessment. The same is true of streets, and the paving and improvement of gravel roads. Special assessments will be based upon the value of your property and the cost of improvements. The practice usually followed by municipalities is to permit the land-owner to complete his payments over a period of five or ten years, but to allow him a bonus or reduction if payment is made prior to the expiration of the five or ten year period.

For example, a resort city near New York, entering upon a beach rehabilitation project, required landowners whose property was assessed at five thousand dollars to pay a special charge or assessment of six hundred dollars, payable over a ten year period. This amounted to a twelve percent assessment or one and two-tenths percent a year, with interest at two percent a year on the unpaid portion, and with a discount of ten percent if paid in full during the first year, nine percent if paid in full during the second year, and so forth.

While you should not buy a house if there is any danger of your losing it, or of not being able to pay your taxes on time, you should ascertain the dates on which taxes are payable, and the penalties attached to late payment. As a rule, your tax bill will be mailed to you two months before the due date, but if you fail to pay by the last date, your penalty, at the rate of seven percent, will accrue from a date one month prior to the last date allowed for payment. If your defaults are substantial, and continue for any length of time, the authorities may sell the tax lien.

Taxes usually are payable in two equal installments, six months apart, although this practice is subject to local variations and you may learn that your taxes are payable in one, three or four instalments. Furthermore, your village or town tax and your county or school district tax may be payable at different times, thus permitting you to "stagger" your payments.

(3) *Financing a Mortage*: The fact that you have only a comparatively small amount of cash available need not mean that you are precluded from owning your own home. Any young or middle-aged person or couple can purchase a home commensurate with their earning ability.

If you can provide cash equal to ten per cent of the price of the house you want to buy, let your lawyer get busy. He will prepare a contract for the purchase of the property, and will include a clause, which will permit you to withdraw it if for any reason a mortgage cannot be obtained.

The usual practice is for you to deposit a mutually agreed upon deposit on the signing of the contract, with a provision that this is to be forfeited if the deal is not completed. This provision is made to make good to the seller any damages he may sustain through having withdrawn his property from the market for the duration of the contract. After the contract is signed, your lawyer will present you with a printed form of application for a mortgage. The mortgage will be a bank or an insurance company. An individual mortgagee, as a rule, has no printed forms.

You will be thoroughly investigated, and your employment record and prospects will be examined. Lending institutions do not want you as a mortgagor unless (1) your property is worth as much or more than the amount of the mortgage, and (2) you can meet your payments when due.

The rule of thumb is that you should not spend more than twenty-five percent of your income for housing, and the lending institution will prefer an arrangement under which your monthly payments will not exceed your weekly salary or earnings. The larger your cash payment, the smaller your monthly payments. After your cash payment is made to the seller, you will execute a mortgage for the balance to the lending institution, which will give you a check for the amount of the mortgage. In exchange for your deed, you will endorse the check to the seller, who will then be out of the transaction.

Your mortgage will be for a term long enough to give you plenty of time to pay. Mortgages run for as long as twenty-five or thirty years. In general, the mortgage should be cleared up by sixty years of age. Mortgages on older property may run only for fifteen or twenty years. The longer your mortgage, the smaller your monthly payments.

Your monthly payments will be made directly to your mortgagee, who will take care of all other details. The mortgagee, to protect its loan, must be certain that the taxes are paid, and that the insurance is maintained. Consequently, the mortgagee will pay the taxes, and insurance premiums, and will collect from you each month a sum sufficient to pay interest, amortization of the loan, taxes, insurance premiums, and water charges.

At first, your interest charges will exceed amortization, and it is only after you have made payments for several years that a larger proportion of your monthly payments will be applied toward amortization. Every time you make a monthly payment, you reduce the unpaid balance of the mortgage. Consequently, a larger part of each succeeding payment is applied toward amortization, and a smaller part toward interest. You can compute for yourself the reduced monthly payments which you can effect by paying a proportionately larger amount of cash, or by making a lump sum payment at any time during the life of the mortgage.

F. MORTGAGES IN GENERAL

A mortgage is very much like a deed. Sometimes it is referred to as a deed by the mortgagor or borrower to the mortgagee or lender, delivered on condition that if the money is repaid by the borrower, the deed is to be of no effect. However, title remains in the mortgagor or borrower.

Under such circumstances, the form of a mortgage is almost the same as that of a deed, although there are different provisions to protect the rights of the parties, particularly of the lender or mortgagee, whose money is tied up in the property while it remains under the control of the mortgagor or borrower.

G. PURCHASE MONEY MORTGAGE

The Vendor may be willing to take the position of a lender, and to permit you to pay part of the purchase price by executing a purchase money mortgage in lieu of cash. If there is another mortgage on the premises, the purchase money mortgage will, of course, be a second mortgage, and will be subordinate to the pre-existing mortgage. On the other hand, if there is no pre-existing mortgage, the purchase money mortgage will take priority over any other mortgage subsequently executed. The purchase money mortgage will be drawn by the seller's attorney. If the mortgage is an ordinary bank mortgage, it will be drawn by the attorneys for the bank. Purchase money mortgages are no longer as common as formerly, and today are accepted somewhat reluctantly. If you are buying a home, and are a good credit risk, both you and the Vendor will probably prefer to obtain the money from a bank or other lending institution, such as an insurance company or a savings and loan, or building and loan association. Under these circumstances, the loan will be made to you at the time you acquire title, and the proceeds of the loan will be used to pay the balance of the purchase price.

In addition to mortgage transactions, which take place at the time a home is purchased, a mortgage may be made to raise money for improving or rehabilitating a house to meet extraordinary expenses, to go into business, or to pay for the education of your children. The older your house, the more difficulty you may encounter in obtaining a mortgage.

Although the land itself is the security for the loan, almost any lender will ask you to sign a bond, by the terms of which you agree to pay the indebtedness if the property should be insufficient to satisfy the loan.

H. FORMS

The form of a mortgage is sometimes provided by Statute and may be as follows:

1. This mortgage, made the 11*th* day of *August*, nineteen
2. hundred and *seventy-nine*, between EMMETT O'CONNELL, re
3. *siding at* 1798 *Liberty Drive, New York, New York,* the mort-
4. gagor, and GEORGE MALONE, *residing at* 100 *Park Avenue,*
5. *New York, New York,* the mortgagee.
6. Witnesseth, that to secure the payment of an indebtedness
7. in the sum of *twenty-five thousand* ($25,000.00) dollars, lawful money
8. of the United States to be paid on the 10*th* day of *August*
9. nineteen hundred and *ninety-four,* with interest thereon to be
10. computed from *August* 11*th,* 1979, at the rate of *eight* (8%)
11. per centum per annum, and to be paid *quarterly,* according to
12. a certain bond or obligation bearing even date herewith, the
13. mortgagor hereby mortgages to the mortgagee *all that lot or*
14. *parcel of land with the buildings and improvements thereon*
15. *in the Borough and County of Queens, City and State of New*
16. *York bounded and described as follows*:
17. BEGINNING *at a point in the westerly line of Delafield Ave-*
18. *nue, distant* 350 *feet southerly, as measured along said west-*
19. *erly line, from the southerly line of West* 246*th Street, as said*

West 246th Street and Delafield Avenue are laid out by the City and shown on Map No. 134 in the Register's Office. Queens County; running thence south 60 degrees, 46 minutes, 49 seconds west, 112.50 feet; thence south 29 degrees, 13 minutes, 11 seconds, east 60 feet; thence north 60 degrees, 46 minutes, 49 seconds east, 112.96 feet to the westerly line of Delafield Avenue, thence northwardly along the westerly line of Delafield Avenue, and on an arc with a radius of 1120 feet. 32.12 feet, and thence north 29 degrees, 13 minutes, 11 seconds west, still along the westerly line of Delafield Avenue, 27.86 feet to the point or place of beginning; excluding however every part of the bed of said Delafield Avenue upon which the above described premises front. The bearings herein are in the system used by the Topographical Bureau, Borough of Queens, for Section 24 of the Final Maps.

And the mortgagor covenants with the mortgagee as follows:

1. That the mortgagor will pay the indebtedness as hereinbefore provided.

2. That the mortgagor will keep the buildings on the premises insured against loss by fire for the benefit of the mortgagee.

3. That no building on the premises shall be removed or demolished without the consent of the mortgagee.

4. That the whole of said principal sum shall become due after default in the payment of any instalment of principal or of interest for *ten days,* or after default in the payment of any tax, water rate or assessment for *thirty* days after notice and demand.

5. That the holder of this mortgage, in any action to foreclose it shall be entitled to the appointment of a receiver.

6. That the mortgagor will pay all taxes, assessments or water rates, and in default thereof, the mortgagee may pay the same.

7. That the mortgagor within *five* days upon request in person or within *ten* days upon request by mail will furnish a statement of the amount due on this mortgage.

8. That notice and demand or request may be in writing

58. and may be served in person or by mail.
59. 9. That the mortgagor warrants the title to the premises.
60. In witness whereof, this mortgage has been duly executed
61. by the mortgagor.
62.   EMMETT O'CONNELL (*Signed*)
63. In presence of
64. JOHN JONES (*Signed*)

STATE OF NEW YORK)
)ss:
COUNTY OF NEW YORK)

On the 11th day of *August,* nineteen hundred and *seventy-nine,* before me personally appeared EMMETT O'CONNELL, to me known, and known to me to be the person described in and who executed the foregoing mortgage, and he duly acknowledged to me that he executed the same.

         GRACE JONES (*Signed*)
         Notary Public, New York County

Lines 1 to 5 include the recital and identification of the parties, while Lines 6 to 12 state the terms of the mortgage. Interest will be computed from the date the money is paid, while the interest rate and the terms of payment are matters to be agreed upon between the borrower and the lender. The description is similar to that contained in the deed.

The covenants further define the obligations of the mortgagor or borrower. In lines 37 and 38 he agrees to pay the indebtedness both as to interest and to principal, while in Lines 39 to 40, he promises to maintain adequate fire insurance. The mortgagee, as a rule, will not be satisfied with a mere promise, but will insist upon holding the policies himself, since the destruction by fire of the building might be equivalent to the destruction of his security, and by holding the policies he is always satisfied of their existence in full force and effect. The demolition or removal clause (Lines 42 and 43), and the default clause (Lines 44 to 48 will permit the mortgagee to exercise his rights in the event of even a minor default, and will not let the mortgagor "get ahead" of the mortgagee to such an extent that security may be endangered or diminished. The provision for the appointment of a receiver (Lines 49 to 50) is for the protection of the mortgagee or lender in the event that foreclosure proceedings should be protracted. If there is any delay in serving a necessary defendant, the foreclosure time may be doubled or tripled, and accrued rents might be paid to the borrower, unless a receiver could be appointed to manage the property, collect the rents, and pay current charges. Without the appointment of the receiver, it might even be possible for the borrower or mortgagor to receive and convert to himself the current income of the property, and at the same time to refuse to pay current obligations which would be a further lien against the mortgagee's security. The tax assessment and water rate clause (Lines 51 to 53) permit the mortgagee to pay and charge to the mortgagor any current obligations which might tend to create a lien against the property. The provisions of Lines 54 to 56 obligate the mortgagor to furnish a statement of amounts due upon the mortgage, while Lines 57 and 58 provide for the service of notice. The amount due may be required if the mortgagee desires to sell the mortgage, and to estop the mortgagor from claiming later that a lesser amount was due.

Let Line 59, governing the warranty of title, serve as a red flag. You should warrant no more title than you have, and if there are any defects or exceptions to your title, be sure that they are listed. If your mortgage is a purchase money mortgage, be sure that the clause reads:

"That the mortgagor warrants only such title as he may have received from the mortgagee by deed of even date."

In addition to the mortgage itself, the mortgagee may require you to sign a bond under which you agree to pay the indebtedness. The form of the bond will be as follows:

1. KNOW ALL MEN BY THESE PRESENTS:
2. That, I, EMMETT O'CONNELL, residing at 1798 *Liberty Drive*
3. *New York, New York,* am held and firmly bound unto
4. GEORGE MALONE residing at 100 *Park Avenue, New York,*
5. *New York* in the sum of *Twenty-five thousand* ($25,000.00) dollars,
6. lawful money of the United States of America, to be paid to
7. the said GEORGE MALONE, his legal representatives or assigns,
8. for which payment, well and truly to be made, I do bind *my-*
9. *self, my heirs,* executors, administrators and assigns firmly by
10. these presents, sealed with *my* seal and dated the *eleventh day*

of *August, nineteen hundred and* seventy-nine.

The condition of the above obligation is such, that if the above obligor, EMMETT O'CONNELL, his legal representatives or assigns, shall well and truly pay or cause to be paid unto GEORGE MALONE, his executors, administrators or assigns, the sum of *Twenty-five thousand ($25,000.00) dollars, to be paid on the tenth day of August, nineteen hundred and ninety-four with interest thereon to be computed from August 11, 1979, at the rate of eight per centum per annum, and to be paid quarterly, and that if the principal amount and such interest computed from the date hereof, at the rate of four per centum per annum on the unpaid balance,* shall be paid with each instalment, then the above obligation to be void, Otherwise to be and remain in full force and virtue.

Th whole of said principal sum shall become due, at the option of said obligee, after default in the payment of *interest for ten (10) days, or payment of instalment of principal for ten (10) days, or after default for thirty (30) days in the payment* of any tax or assessment which may be levied or imposed upon the premises described in the mortgage collateral to this bond.

The holder of this bond and the mortgage collateral thereto, in any action to foreclose the same, shall be entitled without any notice and without regard to the adequacy of any security for the debt or the solvency of the mortgagor or other persons liable therefor, to the appointment of a receiver of the rents and profits of the land and premises embraced in the said mortgage, and said rents and profits are hereby assigned to the holder of this bond and the mortgage that accompanies it, in the event of any default in paying said principal or interest, or taxes levied against the premises described in said mortgage.

                            EMMETT O'CONNELL *(Signed)*

Sealed and delivered in the presence of

JOHN JONES *(Signed)*

STATE OF NEW YORK)
)ss:
COUNTY OF NEW YORK)

On the *eleventh* day of *August,* nineteen hundred and

seventy-nine before me personally came EMMETT O'CONNELL to me known and known to me to be the individual described in, and who executed the foregoing instrument, and acknowledged that he executed the same.

GRACE JONES (*Signed*)
Notary Public, New York County

The bond requires little explanation. If you pay the mortgage, it is to be of no effect, otherwise you will be held for the full amount.

Chapter 3

CONTRACTING FOR PURCHASING AND BUYING REAL ESTATE

A. THE IMPORTANCE AND FUNCTION OF THE CONTRACT

The usual procedure in a real estate transaction is for the Purchaser to inspect the property, give a small deposit, and a few days later, sign a contract and pay a larger deposit. In the contract itself a date will be fixed for the "closing of title" or delivery of the deed, and at such time, the balance of the purchase price will be paid. As a rule the "closing of title" is from thirty to ninety days after the date of the contract, although this intervening period may be as short as a week and as long as three or four months. This procedure may vary and in some situations, payments on account may be made after the date of the contract and prior to the closing.

The importance of having your lawyer prepare the contract, or examine the contract which you are to sign, before you deposit your money cannot be over emphasized. All your rights are measured, limited and defined by this contract, and the best lawyer in the United States can be of little assistance, if you have signed a contract which compels you to take an unmarketable title or to take a house which upon closer scrutiny is one that you do not want at all. If any serious difficulty requiring litigation should arise between the Vendor and the Purchaser, the outcome of the litigation will be determined primarily by the clauses in the contract. Postponement, until the closing of title, of the problems which ordinarily arise in real estate transactions is rarely a satisfactory solution. Each transaction requires its own contract. While printed forms are used, they seldom, if ever, cover adequately the situation at hand, and the variety of questions arising require their own peculiar answer.

If you intend to sell property, have your lawyer prepare a contract and keep it available. When the prospective purchaser arrives, let him sign the contract. As a purchaser, give as small a deposit as possible to protect yourself against loss if the deal should fall through. Let your lawyer sit down with the Vendor's lawyer and decide just what you want to do. Your lawyer will know your problems and will be able to bargain with the Vendor's lawyer and to arrange for the inclusion of the mutually satisfactory provisions which are essential to a fair contract.

B. WHAT THE REAL ESTATE CONTRACT MEANS

(1) *The Date*: the first words in the contract will be "Agreement made this   day of   , 19......." The date should be filled in at the time the contract is signed. In almost all jurisdictions, contracts may be executed on Sunday. Under no circumstances, omit the date merely because the date is a Sunday. Where time limitations are fixed, the date may be of the utmost importance, and your inadvertent omission may cause you considerable expense later on.

(2) *The Parties To The Contract*: The person owning and selling the property is referred to as the "Vendor," while the buyer or purchaser is simply referred to as the "Purchaser." While the words "Seller" and "Buyer" are also used, they apply more specifically to buyers and sellers of Personal Property, and the terms "Vendor" and "Purchaser" refer more specifically to the parties involved in real estate transactions.

Immediately after the date, the contract will proceed with the words "between Casper Budness residing at 182 Highball Street, Wilmington, Delaware, as Vendor (or seller) and John Gaffney residing at 323 Admiral Street, Chicago, Illinois, as Purchaser." If Casper Budness is married, provide in the contract that his wife will join in the deed. For all you know, he may have been married before dower was abolished, and a deed without his wife's consent will then be ineffective to transfer her rights to the property, if he should predecease her. On the other hand, if John Gaffney is a young man and you believe that he may not be of full age, include a warranty by John that he is of full age, capable of entering into the transaction. The proper words will be "John Gaffney, as Purchaser, warranting that he is of full age."

Be careful not to enter into a contract with anyone who has been declared by a Court to be an incompetent, and if you deal with an executor or agent, satisfy yourself as to his authority by examining a certified copy of the Will or the agent's power of attorney. If you deal with a corporation obtain some assurance that the corporation is empowered to act and that a resolution of the stockholders is not necessary. For your protection, include a specific warranty to the effect that John Gaffney, as President of the Seafarers Society, Inc., warrants that this transaction has been approved by a majority of the stockholders of the corporation. If you are dealing with a partnership, insist upon the signature of each partner, since you cannot tell, without examining the deed which transferred the property to the partnership, whether the partners hold the property as tenants in common or as joint tenants.

(3) *Description of The Property*: The next provision in the contract states that

> "The Vendor agrees to sell and convey, and the Purchaser agrees to purchase all . . ."

here will be inserted the description of the property. There is no prescribed form as long as the property is described with sufficient detail to permit its ready identification. Do not rely on street numbers, which may be changed from time to time.

If you plan to obtain a mortgage, a survey will be necessary in any event, and it is well to have this survey incorporated into the description to insure an accurate report of just what property is to pass. Your lawyer will usually map out the description and check his written description against the survey. If the property is included or is located on a map, he will refer to the map in specific terms, such as

> "The said property being the same premises known as lots numbers 4 and 5, on a map entitled 'Map of Long Beach West Estates, J. S. Vanderberg, Civil Engineer, filed in the Office of the Clerk of the County of Nassau, as map number 182 on May 14, 1919'."

If any monuments, stone or metal markers or landmarks are used to limit or assist in the description, they will be described in detail, such as

"North one hundred twenty (120) feet to a white marble monument"

or to
"a white stone marker"

or to
"the center of a large rock"

or even
"to an oak tree approximately one hundred seventy-five (175) feet from the point or place of beginning."

We have seen, in the Chapter on Deeds, how streets can be used to describe property, but extreme care should be taken that the course of the street has not changed, that it has not been widened, or that its name has not been changed. A description by lot and block upon a map which shows streets usually conveys an easement in the streets even if the streets are those of a private development. If however, you are buying property which abuts on a river or a lake, be sure that the description in your contract is sufficiently broad to cover your riparian rights. Just as your description should include a clause reading

"together with all the right, title and interest of the Vendor in the land lying in the street in front of and adjoining said premises, to the center line thereof,"

the description of riparian rights should read

"Together with all rights of the seller to the land now below the surface of Lake Arrowhead."

"Together with the right to enter upon or into the said Railpole River for any purpose whatsoever and together with the title of the Vendor to the land beneath the survey of the said river to the center thereof."

If the description is not sufficiently broad, you may find yourself precluded from exercising the rights of a riparian owner and you may be limited to merely looking at the water. Have your lawyer examine the contract to be sure that you get what you bargain for.

(4.) *Personal Property*: When you buy a house, your receiving the refrigerator, the stove, the electric light fixtures, the shades, storm windows, screens, etc., will be an important consideration. We have already discussed just what is and what is not personal property, and you should be as specific as possible in enumerating the items of personal property which are to be included in the sale. The mere statement of

"Together with the appurtenances"

may not be sufficiently definite to bind the Vendor to give you what you want and, on the other hand, if you are the Vendor, it may subject you to giving away something which you had not intended to include in the sale. What personal property constitutes appurtenances may vary from state to state and it is, therefore, important to include a specific description of just what you wish to acquire. If you are the seller, and wish to sell only the house without any of its detachable personal property, strike from the description in the contract the word "appurtenances." You may then be in a position to be as generous or as niggardly as you choose. On the other hand, if you are the Purchaser, do not be content with the mere word "appurtenances" but insist on a clause that states

"included in this sale and warranted to be owned by the vendor free from any liens or other incumbrances are all furniture or articles of personal property attached to, or contained in, or used in connection with the said premises including specifically but not exclusively all appurtenances, fixtures, stoves, ice boxes, refrigerators, awnings, screens, shades, storm winddows, plants and shrubbery."

Even this may not be sufficient. If the property is of a special nature and if you have examined the specific items which you want, a better clause is

"Included in this sale and warranted to be owned by the seller, free from any incumbrances or liens, are all articles of personal property more specifically described in schedule A annexed to, and made a part of this agreement."

In Schedule A, you should list every specific item of property. This may run into several pages, but then suppose you are buying a summer bungalow which is to be sold to you "furnished and ready for occupancy." What "furnished and ready for occupancy" means to you and the Vendor may not be quite the same. Do you want it to include shades, china, silverware, shower curtains and the thousand and one large and small items which make the summer cottage livable? If you do not list them one by one, Mrs. Vendor may decide that her husband had no business selling that table which she bought at an auction four years ago, and you may move in to find yourself eating your dinner from the cupboard instead of the table which was carted away by Mrs. Vendor shortly before her husband surrendered the keys to you.

(5) *Fuel*: Closely allied to personal property is the question of the oil, coal or wood on the premises at the time of the closing of title. This may be so insignificant that the seller is willing to disregard it but, on the other hand, he may have ordered a full winter's supply of coal before selling the house. He may even have filled his coal bin or his oil tank early in the summer and then before cold weather sets in, he may have decided suddenly to sell his house. Having a fairly substantial amount of money tied up in fuel, he will insist upon the following clause:

"Purchaser agrees to pay the Seller, in addition to the purchase price set forth herein, the cost price to the Vendor of oil on the premises on the day before the delivery of the deed. An estimate of the amount of oil, on the premises at such time shall be furnished by the Vendor."

The Purchaser, on the other hand, should not bind himself to pay the cost price but if he is to pay for the fuel, should bind himself only to pay

"The cost price thereof to the Vendor or the market price on the day of closing whichever may be the lower."

Either party may also desire to specify a reliable fuel dealer or expert to make the estimate, and the clause may read:

"The written estimate of Jack G. Brown, of Brown-Marco, Inc., as to the value and amount of fuel on hand at the date of closing shall be accepted as conclusive by the parties."

(6) *Crops*: It is best to specify just what crops or what vegetation is to pass with the property. Trees, of course, until they have

been severed from the land, are real property but there may be some question where the trees are small saplings, planted so close together that it is obvious that they are intended to be transplanted later on. If one consideration in your purchase of the property is the growing crop, have your lawyer include a provision in the description of the deed to the effect that

> "Included in this sale and warranted by the Vendor to be free from liens or mortgages are all growing crops and all items of vegetation not harvested at the date of this contract."

If there is any possibility that the closing of title may be delayed, include a provision

> "At any time after the date of this agreement, the purchaser may enter upon the said premises for the purpose of harvesting or removing any crops, plants or vegetation of any nature growing on the said premises."

If you are the Vendor, be sure that the down payment has been sufficiently large to cover the value of the crop.

(7) *Incumbrances and Defects of Title*:

(a) *General*: Rural property may have been held by one family for years, and may have a few restrictions in prior deeds, with no question as to its limitations, descriptions, or surveys. On the other hand, city property often presents an altogether different picture. Very few titles to city property are entirely clear, although in most instances the defects are not sufficiently great to prevent a ready transfer. After the property is described, the contract may contain a clause to the effect

> "The said property is sold, subject to the following:"

The incumbrances or defects, subject to which the sale is made will then be listed. They may include "exceptions to the survey," encroachments, mortgages, covenants, and restrictions in prior deeds, violations, leases, occupancy of tenants, rent or other regulations, zoning restrictions or easement.

(b) *Survey Exceptions and Encroachments*: The contract prepared by the vendor's attorney will probably contain a clause

> "The premises are sold subject to any state of facts which an accurate survey may show."

If you are selling your property and have not had a survey for some time, this is a very good clause, but if you are on the other side of the transaction and are about to buy property, beware of any such sweeping description. It is best to expand the clause as follows:

"Subject to any state of facts which an accurate survey may show, provided the title is not thereby rendered unmarketable."

As a buyer, you probably will not want to accept an unmarketable title. As a seller, however, you may not know whether or not your title is unmarketable, since this often is a complicated question, both of law and of fact, and you may merely say to the prospective purchaser, "Here is my property. Decide for yourself whether it is marketable." If a survey is available, a compromise may be arrived at by stating that the premises are sold

"subject to any state of facts revealed by the survey annexed to this agreement and initialed by both parties:"

Encroachments may be of three kinds.
(1) Upon a public highway
(2) Upon the adjoining property
(3) A building on the adjoining property encroaching upon the land which is the subject of the contract.

Many states have passed statutes to provide relief against hardship resulting from an inadvertent encroachment. Before you sign the contract, your lawyer, who will be familiar with local regulations, will provide the particular safeguard which is required in the case of the property which you are buying. When an encroachment is discovered, consider yourself not in the light of the purchaser, but as a vendor who a few years later may be in the position of attempting to dispose of the property. A few years hence you may saddled with a white elephant. What constitutes a marketable title is a question of law which can be answered by your lawyer. Give him all the facts and be guided by his considered judgment.

(c) *Mortgages*: The vendor's attorney will probably present you with a contract stating that the premises are sold

"Subject to mortgages and incumbrances of record."

As the purchaser, you should insist that these mortgages be described specifically and will ask that the clause read

"Subject to a mortgage now a lien upon the premises and recorded in the Office of the Clerk of the County of Nassau, in Liber 321 of mortgages, Page 168."

Regardless of your unbounded confidence in the integrity of the vendor, insist upon a specific list of mortgages. Mortgages and restrictions of record may sometimes be difficult to find, and may be overlooked. There is also the danger that a mortgage may be executed prior to the contract and may be recorded subsequent thereto. In such a case, you may be bound to accept the premises subject to such mortgage.

Do not agree to assume payment of an existing mortgage. You will, of course, be required to take title "subject to existing mortgages." The land itself will be the mortgagee's security. However, if you assume the mortgage and the property is destroyed, washed away in a flood, or if it diminishes in value, the mortgagee may look to you to make good the deficiency.

Provide for the production of some evidence of the reduction of the mortgage and proof of the amount still due. For complete protection, the clause should read

"Subject to a mortgage now a lien of record, recorded in the office of the Clerk of the County of Westchester, in Volume 177 of Mortgages, Page 323, upon which the vendor warrants that the unpaid balance does not exceed the principal sum of five thousand four hundred twenty-eight ($5,428.00) dollars, with an interest at eight (8%) percent from March 15th, 1979."

Also provide that

"At the time of the delivery of the deed, the vendor will produce a certificate executed and acknowledged by the mortgagee in form for recording, certifying the amount of the unpaid interest and principal, date of maturity, and the rate of interest thereon, and the vendor will pay all fees and taxes for the recording of such certificate."

If you are selling your property, try not to bind yourself to such a stringent provision, since you may encounter some unforeseen difficulty in obtaining a certificate fromm the mortgagee, and your failure to produce a certicate may open the door to a rejection of title.

(d) *Covenants and Restrictions*: If the contract is prepared by the vendor's attorney, it will probably contain a provision that the property is sold

"Subject to covenants, restrictions, and easements contained in prior instruments of record."

or

'Subject to covenants and restrictions of record."

If your own lawyer, representing you as the purchaser, sees such a provision, he will immediately ask that there be added to this statement the words

"provided title is not thereby rendered unmarketable."

The vendor's attorney will argue that this provision is too broad, since he is willing to sell what he has but no more. One of two compromises will probably be reached, the first of which, more favorable to the vendor, will provide that the premises are being sold subject to

"Covenants and restrictions contained in a deed recorded in the office of the County Clerk of Clallam County, in Liber 22 of your Conveyances, at Page 405."

If your attorney has not seen the deed, he may insist that it be made part of and be annexed to the contract. On the other hand, the vendor's attorney may argue he is merely selling the premises as they are, and reports that the present use does not violate any of the covenants. He will therefore suggest the following provision:

"subject to covenants, restrictions and easements of record provided that such restrictions, covenants and easements do not prohibit the present structure on the premises, and the continued use of the premises for the purposes for which they are now employed."

An easement is a right of an owner of land to use the land of another for a special purpose not inconsistent with the general property of the owner. An everyday example is a common driveway between two neighboring houses, partly on the land of each. Each owner has an easement in the other's land.

Be careful of easements. If there are easements which are not matters of record, incorporate them into the contract by way of warranty, so that you can hold the vendor and obtain a proportionate diminution of the price if they are serious or more extensive than you anticipated.

(e) *Violations*: If the contract is silent on the question of violations, as a purchaser you will be required to accept the property subject to any violations, whether or not a ntoice of violation has been served upon the vendor. As a purchaser, you should insist upon the removal of all violations and should ask that the following clause be included in the contract:

> "All notices of violation of law or municipal ordinances, orders or requirements issued by or recorded in the office of any state or municipal department, and which affect the premises at the date of the closing, shall be complied with and removed by the vendor and the premises shall be conveyed free of the same. The provision shall survive the delivery of the deed hereunder."

The vendor will object violently to such a provision. He may even offer to permit you to inspect the premises and to list any violations to give him a chance to correct them. This may be costly to him, since it may require the erection of a fire escape, and at times may reduce a building from a three-family to a two-family dwelling. The vendor may even ask that the effective date of violations be fixed at the date of the agreement and not at the date of closing, or may provide that objections be served upon the vendor ten or fifteen days prior to the closing. If there is some serious question, a cancellation clause may be incorporated into the contract, providing

> "If the reasonable cost of removal of violations shall exceed one thousand five hundred ($1,500.00) dollars (or any other mutually acceptable figure) the vendor shall have the right and option to cancel this agreement upon refunding to the purchaser the amount previously paid under this contract."

This situation is much more serious in a multiple dwelling than in a one or two-family house, but it is one that should not be overlooked. Even in small houses, compliance with fire and safety regulations may be expensive or extremely difficult, particularly during times when building materials are difficult to obtain.

(f) *Leases and Tenancies*: In the present housing market, possession is of the essence in the sale of a one or two-family house. If the contract is silent, the vender is under an obligation to deliver possession at the time of the delivery of the deed. If he does not protect himself by providing that the premises are sold subject to occupancy by a tenant, he may be liable for damages and may be required to pay the cost of housing the purchaser until possession is actually obtained. The usual provision desired by sellers is that the premises are sold

"subject to existing leases and tenancies."

If you are a purchaser, do not accept the premises subject to existing leases and tenancies, unless you know exactly what they are. Under present conditions, a veteran purchasing a home for his own occupancy is usually allowed to evict the occupant, but it may take him anywhere from two to eighteen months to effect such an eviction. Even a "sure fire" law suit may take considerable time and money.

A more equitable provision is

"subject to leases and tenancies as set forth in Schedule A annexed hereto and made part thereof."

If the property in question is merely a one family house, the provision may read as follows:

"subject to occupancy of the premises by Philip Cohen as a month to month tenant at a monthly rental of three hundred ($300.00) dollars."

The purchaser should examine carefully every lease. Occasionally leases contain peculiar provisions obligating the landlord to make extensive repairs, to provide unusual services, such as excessive heat and hot water, or extraordinary frequent garbage removal, and may provide for penalties in the event of fire, or condemnation of the premises by the government. Furthermore, a lease is not necessarily conclusive, since the parties may have a subsequent agreement for a larger or smaller rent. It is better for the purchaser to provide that

> "the vendor warrants that the leases examined and initialed by the purchaser are in full force and effect."

If the tenancy is a month to month tenancy under an oral lease, insert a statement that

> "The premises are to be conveyed subject to the month to month tenancy of Philip Cohen, which tenancy is warranted by the vendor to be a month to month tenancy, terminable on thirty (30) days notice, at a monthly rental of three hundred ($300.00) dollars."

Pay particular attention to any provisions providing for the deposit of security under a lease. If the landlord is obligated to repay the security, it should be deducted from the purchase price. There may also be some doubt as to whether the security may be transferred and the provisions of the local law which apply should be investigated carefully before the provision is finally selected.

The sale and the occupancy will, of course, be subject to rent control regulations, and wherever possible originals and certified copies of the pertinent orders in effect should be annexed to the agreement.

(8.) *Marketable Titles and Insurable Titles*: In the absence of any provisions, the Vendor is obliged to convey a "marketable title." A marketable title has been defined as one which is so clearly a good title that the Courts will compel its acceptance by a Purchaser.

While it may be argued that Courts, being composed of human beings, may vary, there are certain broad principles within which all will agree. No Court will compel a Purchaser to accept as "marketable" a title which may later be defeated, whether such defeat may be occasioned by encroachments, the foreclosure of an outstanding lien, or the assertion of a superior claim.

After you sign the contract for the purchase of your house or your vacant land, your lawyer will "search the title." His first step will be to ascertain the names of the owners of the property for the past thirty years, read their deeds, and decide whether there are any valid objections to or defects in the title. The property may have been described improperly in an earlier deed, or the name of the grantee may have been misspelled.

If no such defects are encountered, your lawyer will next look for mortgages, and satisfy himself that there are no unsatisfied mortgages outstanding. Thereafter, he will look for mechanics,' liens, a lis pendens (a pending foreclosure action), bankruptcies by any former owner, conditional sale contracts, and judgments against any former owners. Having completed this search, your lawyer will next examine the records at the tax offices, to be sure that there are no unpaid taxes or assessments, and will also examine the records of the Department of Water Supply or, if water is furnished by a private company, the records of the company. The last item searched will, of course, be violations, which will be listed in the appropriate municipal department.

A marketable title and an insurable title are not necessarily the same. A title may be marketable, yet a title insurance company may refuse to insure it, because it fears the expense of a lawsuit to defend the title. This may be so even though the title is one which cannot be defeated. On the other hand, a title company may, under some circumstances, be willing to insure a title which, because of some minor defect, is not marketable. Do not permit yourself to be bound to a provision which requires you to accept an "insurable title" or, worst of all, one which binds you to accept a title which a specific title company will insure. As a purchaser, insist on a clause to the effect that

"The Vendor shall deliver a marketable title of record."

As Vendor, try to limit your obligations to what you know you can convey.

(9) *The Purchase Price*: The part of the contract which will be the most important to both the Vendor and the Purchaser will be that which concerns the purchase price. The entire price will not be paid until the delivery of the deed, and will usually be in the following form:

The purchase price for the said premises is Sixty thousand ($60,000.00) dollars, payable as follows:

a. Five hundred ($500.00) dollars deposit paid on the twenty-first day of January, 1979, receipt of which has heretofore been acknowledged.

b. Five thousand ($5,000.00) dollars on the signing of this contract, the receipt of which is hereby acknowledged (by check subject to collection) (in cash) (by certified check).

c. Ten thousand ($10,000.00) dollars in cash or certified check drawn on a Cleveland, Ohio, bank on the delivery of the deed.

d. Eleven thousand ($11,000.00) dollars by taking title subject to a mortgage in the said amount now a lien against the said premises, and recorded in the offices of the County Clerk of the County of Cuyahoga, in Liber 188 of Mortgages at Page 234.

e. Six thousand ($6,000.00) dollars by the Purchaser executing, acknowledging and delivering his bond in the said sum, to be secured by a purchase money mortgage on the said premises, bearing interest at the rate of nine (9%) percent from the date of delivery of the deed, to be executed and recorded at the expense of the Purchaser.

This provision is probably more complicated than that which is encountered in most contracts. All will state the total purchase price, but there will not necessarily have been a payment prior to the execution of the contract. If no such payment was made, subparagraph "a" will of course be omitted. Paragraph "b" will contain the amount of cash or down payment to be made at the time of the execution of the contract. As a Purchaser, you should try to make this as small as possible. If the title should prove to be defective, or if for any other reason the transaction is not consummated, you will want as little money as possible tied up. As a rule, if you obtain a mortgage, the lending institution will prefer to have you deposit twenty (20%) percent of the total price, although in some cases ten (10%) percent will suffice. The Vendor should, of course, insist upon the down payment being as large as the traffic will bear, since there will then be ample funds to pay any damages sustained if the Purchaser defaults. It is important to the Vendor to receive this down payment in cash or by certified check. If he accepts an uncertified check, he may in effect be giving the Purchaser an option, since the latter may change his mind and stop payment on the check prior to its clearing. The Purchaser, on the other hand, may wish to avoid the bother of obtaining cash or a certified check, and may argue that if Vendor suspects that the check is not good, he should not do business with the Purchaser in the first place.

The Vendor should insist on cash or a certified check at the time of the delivery of the deed, since he is then parting irrevocably with his property. He should also insist that the certified check be drawn on a bank in the immediate vicinity of the property, to permit verification and quick clearance. If the Purchaser's account is maintained in a bank somewhat distant from the scene of the closing, the closing date should be set sufficiently far in advance to give him an opportunity to transfer his funds to a local bank.

If the premises are mortgaged at the time of the sale, and you do not have sufficient money to pay off the mortgage, you may take title "subject to" the existing mortgage, or by assuming the existing mortgage or mortgages. If you are a Purchaser, never assume a mortgage unless there is no way to avoid it. On the other hand, if you are a Vendor, try to persuade the Purchaser to assume the mortgage, and the Mortgagee to release you.

If the Purchaser does not have sufficient cash, you may take a purchase money mortgage, which may be either a first or a second mortgage.

(10.) *Risk of Loss Until Closing*: The fairest provisions governing the risk of loss until closing are those found in the Uniform Vendor and Purchaser Risk Act, which has been adopted in Hawaii, Louisiana, Michigan, New York, South Dakota and Wisconsin. In some states in which this act is not in force, the risk of loss is assumed by the Purchaser unless some other provision is made in the contract. Under the Act, when neither title nor possession has been transferred to the Purchaser, and all or a material part of the subject matter of the agreement is destroyed without fault of the Purchaser, or is taken by eminent domain, the Vendor cannot enforce the contract, and the purchaser is entitled to recover any portion of the purchase price which he has paid. If there is a destruction, or taking by eminent domain of an immaterial part of the subject matter, neither party is thereby deprived of the right to enforce the contract, but the purchase price will be reduced proportionately.

On the other hand, the Act provides that when either legal title or possession has been delivered or transferred to the Purchaser, the risk of loss will be borne by the Purchaser, and if the premises are destroyed or are taken by eminent domain, he is still required to pay the full purchase price. In sales where the act is in force, all contracts for the purchase and sale or change of real property will be interpreted in accordance with the act unless the contract itself expressly provides otherwise.

If you are the Purchaser, and want to have the property under any circumstances, include a provision to that effect in your contract, but be sure that you obtain insurance which will be effective as soon as you sign the contract. You may even provide that the insurance in effect shall be maintained by the Vendor for your benefit, but in that case the Vendor probably will ask you to pay the premiums.

The following provision will give you the right to acquire the property under any circumstances:

"In the event of the total or partial destruction of the premises by fire or other casualty prior to the delivery of the deed, the Purchaser may take title subject to such partial or total destruction, and the Vendor shall hold as a trust fund for the Purchaser all sums received under all policies of insurance maintained on the said premises."

If you succeed in inserting such a clause be sure that the premises are in fact insured for their replacement value. You certainly do not want to receive a plot of ground, with the skeleton of a house, and the proceeds of an insurance policy, which, while sufficient before the war, will not provide enough money today to allow you to rebuild one fourth of the house. Ask the Vendor to produce his insurance policies, and refer to them specifically in the agreement. Your clause will then read:

". . . and the Vendor shall hold as a trust fund for the Purchaser all sums received under Fire Insurance Policy Number 514376, issued to the Vendor on July 6, 1945 by the Great Gaffney Fire Insurance Company of California, in the amount of fifteen thousand ($15,000.00) dollars, which policy is warranted by the Vendor to be in full force and effect, with all premiums paid until and including July 6, 19............"

If you are the Vendor, and you permit such a clause, add the words

"The Purchaser will pay to the Vendor, on the delivery of the deed, a sum equal to the premiums on such policy of insurance, from the date of this agreement to the delivery of the deed."

Do not be satisfied to leave to the local custom the important question of risk of loss. The simple clause

"The risk of loss or damage to said premises until the delivery of the deed is assumed by the (Vendor) or (Purchaser)."

will give you some measure of protection.

The law varies greatly from state to state. Consult your lawyer and point out to him just how far you are willing to go to acquire the property.

(11.) *Apportionments*: Whether you are the purchaser of vacant property, a small house or an apartment house, there will be various charges which the Vendor has paid in advance, and others which although not paid may have become a lien on the property. If the apportionment clause does not provide a specific date, the apportionment will be made as of the date that the deed is to be delivered. This is the date usually desired by the Purchaser of vacant land since the expense of carrying the property will then be borne by the Vendor until title actually passes. On the other hand, if the property is a two-family house, or an apartment, or even a one family house whose tenant is paying substantial rent, and who will not vacate the premises as of the date of the closing, the Purchaser may prefer to have the apportionment date advanced to the date of the contract. If the risk of loss is to be assumed by the Purchaser, he will be in a more equitable position to ask that the apportionments be made as of the date of the contract. If the subject matter of the agreement is vacant land, the Vendor will probably argue that the effective date should be the date of the agreement, since any payments by the Vendor after that date will be in effect a reduction of the purchase price.

The apportionment date may hinge upon the period of time which is to elapse between the date of the contract and the delivery of the deed, the delivery of possession, or the stringency of the contract. If there is an escape clause, permitting either party to withdraw in the event of inability to perform, the party who is not given this right or option should receive the benefit of the apportionment date. As a rule, it is customary to declare the date of closing the apportionment date where the property is income producing, and the date of the contract where the property does not produce any revenue.

The usual apportionment clause is as follows:

"The following are to be apportioned (as of date of the closing of title) (as of the date of this agreement):

1. Rents, as and when collected.
2. Interest on mortgages.
3. Insurance premiums.
4. Taxes.
5. Water charges.
6. Rental and service charges on personal property remaining on the premises after the closing of title."

(12.) *Form of Deed*: We have already pointed out that if no particular form of deed is specified in the contract, you will be required to accept a "quitclaim" deed, which will give you, the Vendor's entire "right, title and interest," and nothing more. If you are forced to accept such a deed, ask that the contract also contain a clause to the effect that:

"The obligations of the Vendor shall survive the delivery of the deed, and shall not merge therein."

This clause will protect you against the breach of any warranty or representation made by the Vendor in the contract and, if such a clause is not included, the Vendor's obligations will be extinguished when he delivers the deed. If he delivers a quitclaim deed, his obligation will be extinguished, while if he has given you a bargain and sale deed, you may have recourse only when he himself has been responsible for the creation of a defect in your title. If you are sufficiently fortunate to obtain a full covenant and warranty deed, you need not be particularly concerned about merger. As a rule, however, the Vendor will not deliver a full covenant and warranty deed, and as Purchaser, you should insist on a provision against merger.

The usual clause, with a provision to protect you against mechanics' liens, will be as follows:

"The deed shall be the usual (quitclaim) (bargain and sale) (full covenant and warranty) deed, in proper statutory short form, for recording, duly executed and acknowledged, with Internal Revenue Stamps in the proper amount affixed by the Vendor at the Vendor's expense, so as to convey to the Purchaser the fee simple of the premises, free of all incumbrances and defects, except as stated in this contract, and shall contain a clause to the effect that the Vendor covenants that he will receive the purchase price as a trust fund to be applied first for the purpose of paying the cost of any improvements to the premises, and that such payment will be made before any part of the purchase price is used for any other purpose."

Insist upon this "trust fund" claim. A Vendor cannot, in good faith, object to its inclusion.

(13.) *Purchaser's Liens*: The contract may then contain a clause: "All sums paid on account of this contract and the reasonable expenses of the examination of the title to said premises are hereby made liens thereon, but such liens shall not continue after default by the Purchaser under this contract."

This means that if, for any reason, the Vendor cannot or will not deliver a deed giving a clear title, he must not only return the deposit paid but must also pay whatever expenses the Purchaser incurred in examining the title. Any payments made by the Purchaser then becomes a lien on the property, similar to a mortgage, so if the Vendor refuses or is unable to return the money which he has received on account, the property may be sold and the Purchaser reimbursed from the proceeds of the sale. While the seller cannot have any reasonable objection to this provision insofar as payments made by the Purchaser are concerned, under present conditions he may object to the clause obligating him to pay for an examination of title, on the theory that he says to the prospective Purchaser, "I will give you what I have, but no more." He may in effect ask the Purchaser to search the title himself, and then decide whether he wants to sign the agreement. In such a situation, he may specifically exclude the expenses of examination of title and may add to the clause the words:

> "Any expenses incurred by the Purchaser for the examination of title are specifically excluded and are the sole responsibility of the Purchaser."

On the other hand, he may concede the reasonableness of the Purchaser's position but may merely ask for the limitation of responsibility by the addition of the words:

> "The Vendor's responsibility for examination of title shall not exceed blank dollars," or

> "The Vendor's responsibility for examination of title shall not exceed the price charged by any title company with offices in the City of Chicago, for the examination of titles in Cook County, Illinois."

The expenses for the examination of titles vary. In some areas a title can be checked for as little as $75, while in other places, an examination may cost as much as $400. If you are a Vendor, know to just what extent you are commiting yourself and limit your responsibility. If you are a Purchaser, know just how far you can go without losing money.

(14) *Time and Place of Closing of Title*: The contract's next clause will probably read:

> "The deed shall be delivered upon receipt of all payments at the office of George Boucek, 2 North La Salle Street, Chicago, Illinois at 2 P. M. on June 15th, 1979."

The deed and the payment of the balance of the purchase price are concurrent conditions, and the Purchaser should avoid any provision which makes payment a condition precedent to the delivery of the deed. The usual place for the closing is the office of the Vendor's attorney and the usual date is from ten to ninety days after the execution of the contract. If a bank or other lending institution is providing the money for a mortgage, the closing will usually be at the offices of the Bank's attorney. In any event the details should be stated with certainty.

If no provision is made, time is not considered to be "of the essence," or of the utmost importance. If you are the Purchaser and you insist that time is of the essence, the Vendor will probably ask that it be made of the essence for both parties since there may be objections to title. If you believe that you may encounter difficulty in obtaining the mortgage, you should provide for an adjournment of the closing. The time clause may read:

> "Time of performance under this contract is of the essence to both parties. The Vendor at the request of the Purchaser agrees to adjourn the closing of title, delivery of the deed and payment of the balance of the purchase price for a period not exceeding forty-five days. The Purchaser agrees to notify the attorney for the Vendor in writing not later than 10 days before the date herein fixed for the closing of title, of all objections hereunder, to the Vendor's title and agrees to grant the Vendor an adjournment of the closing of title for not more than 45 days to permit the removal or remedy of such defects."

This provision is most important, since either party may be placed in a position where immediate but not eventual performance is difficult and where a slight delay will be sufficient to permit full performance.

(15.) *Naming of Broker*: Be sure that the responsibility for the broker's fees is defined in the contract. Limit your responsibility to one broker, and attempt to place the other party to the contract in a position where he will not be able to assist a different broker in claiming commissions. For instance, you may have listed your property with your own broker only to find yourself confronted with a suit by another broker who claimed that he introduced the Purchaser to you. If the second broker happens to be a friend of the Purchaser, you realize that as Vendor you may be in for an uncomfortable law suit. From the Vendor's point of view, the provision should read as follows:

> "The Purchaser represents to the Vendor that this sale was brought about by James J. Gallagher, as broker and that no other broker was instrumental in bringing about this sale."

The Purchaser will then ask that there be added the words:

> "The Vendor shall pay the brokerage commission to James J. Gallagher, if and when title passes hereunder."

The Purchaser should insist upon the Vendor's assumption of liability for commission.

Occasionally, as Purchaser, you may be confronted with a request for additional safeguards. Whatever they are, you should consent to them only after your attorney has seen them.

(16.) *Modification or Changes after the Signing of Contract*: Suppose that after the contract is signed, you and the Vendor discover there are several matters concerning which a modification is desirable. Do not merely rely on each other's good faith. Even the best of friends are much better off when their agreements are reduced to writing and faulty recollection will have no chance to create confusion. You will be much better off to exchange letters and to include a clause to the effect that:

"This contract may not be changed orally and may be modified only by an agreement in writing signed by the parties against whom enforcement of any modification, change or waiver is sought."

(17.) *Inability to Perform*: Suppose that after you have signed your contract the Vendor reports to you that he is unable to give you a clear title, or that he is unable to deliver possession. What are your remedies? As we previously pointed out, your rights and remedies will be governed strictly by the contract which you have signed. Provide in your contract for such a contingency. If you want the property under any circumstances, or if you yourself want the option of deciding whether you still continue, include a clause reading as follows:

"If for any reason the title to said premises shall prove unmarketable, the Purchaser shall have option of (a) cancelling and abrogating this agreement, in which event the same shall be null and void without further claim by either party against the other, except that the Vendor shall repay to the Purchaser the amounts theretofore paid to the Vendor hereunder, together with the actual net expenses which the Purchaser may have incurred for the examination of the title, or (b) taking title subject to the default or objection with a proportionate diminution in the purchase price to be determined by agreement of the Vendor, Purchaser and a third party to be selected by the Vendor and Purchaser. In the event that the Vendor and Purchaser are unable to agree, within three days, upon the appointment of a third party, either party may apply to any Court of competent jurisdiction for the appointment of a third party."

The Vendor will probably object to such a clause and will argue that you should either take the title or reject it. He may assent to the clause as long as you limit the words of "b" to read "take title subject to the default or objection."

On the other hand, you may be in a position where at the time you sign the contract you are not sure that you can obtain a mortgage, and without a mortgage you may not have sufficient money to consummate the deal. The vendor will probably insist on some forfeit being posted to reimburse him for having withdrawn his property from the market and you will of course realize the fairness of his position. On the other hand, the vendor may suffer no damage whatsoever, and in such event you may provide for the refund of the money to you with allowances to be made to the Vendor for the expenses incurred for his attorney. An appropriate clause will be

"If, in the event that the Purchaser shall be unable to obtain a mortgage covering the premises, or shall be unable to pay the purchase price as provided in this agreement, the same shall be cancelled and abrogated without further claim by either party against the other, except that the Vendor shall repay to the Purchaser the amounts theretofore paid to the Vendor hereunder, less attorney's fees of $50 incurred by the Vendor."

If the only details to be investigated at the time you sign the contract are those of the title itself, you need not be particularly concerned on this point. However, if there is any probability of difficulty in raising the necessary funds, do not trust to luck but be sure that an appropriate provision is included.

(18.) *Permission to the Purchaser to Enter the Premises*: If you are the Vendor, your attorney will undoubtedly recommend that your possession clause read:

"The Purchaser shall not enter into or upon the premises, nor assume possession thereof, for any purpose whatsoever, prior to the delivery of the deed hereunder. Possession shall be delivered by the Vendor simultaneously with the closing of title."

Any other course followed by the Vendor is an invitation to litigation. Once the Purchaser has taken possession, he may be reluctant to leave, and Courts under some circumstances may be even more reluctant to evict him. Furthermore, he may install some improvements, and may find himself in a position to file a mechanic's lien against the property, thus holding up a sale to any other party.

On the other hand, you may be a Purchaser who is desperate for a place to live, and may want to use the 30 or 60 days intervening between the date of contract and the date of closing title to get the house ready for your family. If the Vendor refuses to let you enter for fear of the consequences of a cancellation of the contract, you may placate him by offering a clause reading:

"The Purchaser may enter upon the premises solely for the purpose of effecting repairs to which the Vendor may have consented in writing. All such repairs shall be at the expense of and at the risk of the Purchaser who agrees to permit his down payment to be held by the Vendor as security against any liens which may be filed against the Purchaser by reason of such repairs."

The Vendor will then be in a position to see that no extensive repairs are performed, and that no work is done which may possibly furnish the basis for a lien too large to be discharged by the money previously paid to the Vendor.

(19.) *Possession*: Possession may be of the essence in the purchase of your house. If immediate possession is important, insert a provision in your contract or provide that

"Possession of the premises at the time of the delivery of the deed is of the essence. If the Vendor is unable to deliver possession, the delivery of the deed may be adjourned for not more than 60 days and if at the end of such time, possession is still unavailable, the Vendor will be deemed to have breached his agreement and all sums paid by the Purchaser shall constitute a lien upon the premises."

The Purchaser may also ask that the words "without affecting his rights to enforce a claim for damages" be included, but it is a rare Vendor who will permit such a clause. We have already explained how difficult it may be to acquire possession. You may be willing to take your chances, but investigate thoroughly, and know just what you are taking, for if possession is unavailable at the time of the delivery of the deed, it is possible that you may be required to wait for as long as two years.

(20.) *Purchase Money Mortgage*: In a great many instances part of the purchase price will be paid by the Purchaser executing and delivering to the Vendor a purchase money bond and mortgage. Under such circumstances, the form of the mortgage is important and should be defined and agreed upon in advance. In States where forms of mortgages are included in the statutes it should be referred to specifically and in any event the purchaser should not be required to guarantee any better title than he receives. Without such a clause you may find yourself in a position of receiving a Bargain & Sale Deed and then warranting your title to your Vendor. To avoid such a situation, provide

> "Said Purchase Money Bond and Mortgage shall contain no unusual clauses; shall be in the statutory short form; and the Purchaser shall be required to warrant only such title as he shall receive from the Vendor."

Since the Mortgage will be drawn by the attorney for the Vendor, his fees, payable by the Purchaser, should be limited. This is particularly important since lawyers' fees vary considerably even in the same town.

Chapter 4
CLOSING TITLE

The observance of the following suggestions will save time and trouble at the closing of title. If the contract of sale does not specify a date for such closing, the law will generally allow a period of from four to six weeks for the the parties involved to meet their respective obligations. The transfer of title is accomplished by delivery of a deed to the buyer. In view of the complexity and importance of a real estate purchase, the buyer should have competent legal representation. In many cases, contracts have been signed, and thereafter, at the closing of title, the services of an attorney have been engaged. In such situations, the buyer may have committed himsel to a contract much to his disadvantage, and it then becomes the lawyer's duty to help extricate his client. Demands cannot be made at this point as a matter of right, from the seller, who has a right to point to the contract and expect full performance. In such cases, the purchaser and his attorney, can only hope and exercise persuasion, so that the buyer's needs may be fulfilled.

Title Search

Prior to closing date, the prospective purchaser should cause a search of title be made by a reputable title company, so as to ascertain whether the seller is able to convey a marketable title. This practise should be followed at all times, even where the buyer is satisfied of the integrity of the seller. The seller may honestly believe that he possesses a sound title, when in fact, the title may be defective. The title search, on the other hand, presents the history and quality of the previous ownership in a record that is indisputable.

The mechanics of such a title search involve the chain of ownership affecting all previous ownership. It includes an examination of each deed of transfer; special attention is given to all descriptions in previous deeds; the size and dimensions of the property purchased is noted, since no prior owner may sell more property than actually owned.

If the search shows, for example, that Jones conveyed to Brown; then Brown to Smith; then White to Buyer, there is a break in chain of title, and a missing link must be accounted for. Under such circumstances, it becomes necessary to check court records for a possible foreclosure; or the records of the Surrogates or Probate Courts to determine whether Smith died during the time of his ownership. In either of such situations, it must be established that Smith's title interest was properly conveyed. If Smith lost his property by means of foreclosure, any defect in such proceedings will prevent the passage of a marketable title. Search will have to be made to determine that all persons who had any interest in Smith's property at the time of foreclosure either as mortgagees, creditors, lien holders were made defendants in such foreclosure proceedings, to establish and decide their rights to the property.

If Smith, on the other hand, died while owning the property, it will be necessary to examine the will, if any, or the court records, to determine whether the executor, or th court appointed administrator, had the right to convey the property, and what is most important, whether all those named as heirs to the property, were notified of their interests and joined in the transfer of the property.

If the history of the title indicates 10 previous owners, each of these must be checked during the period of their ownership, in order to find the existence of possible mortgages, which have not been paid. In many cases, a mortgage previously created and fully discharged by payment, still remains a lien because of failure by a mortgagor, to obtain and file a Satisfaction of Mortgage in the court records. It frequently happens that a mortgage, long since paid, prevents a sale or causes vexatious and expensive delays, because of such failure to record payment. In many instances, the previous mortgagee, who has received payment of the mortgage debt, may have died or his present whereabouts are unknown, the result following, that a Satisfaction of Mortgage is unobtainable. In such a situation, relief might be gained by appeal to the Courts called a Lost Mortgage proceeding, with the consequent loss of time and expense involved, in submitting proof of such payment.

If the search made by the title company indicates that the sellers title is valid, an order should be placed for title insurance, thereby obtaining the guarantee of the insurance company, that in the event of an attack upon the title, at any time, the company will defend such suit or reimburse the buyer for the loss of his home.

Question: In buying a home why do I need an OWNER'S policy of title insurance in addition to the policy that the bank requires when lending me money on a mortgage?

Answer: For the following reasons:

1. The policy required by the bank insures only the bank up to the amount of its mortgage. The amount of cash you have invested in your home, which increases with each payment you make towards the reduction of your mortgage, is unprotected without an OWNER'S policy.
2. When your mortgage is entirely paid off, the bank's insurance ceases and there is no protection at all. An OWNER'S policy continues indefinitely.
3. Attacks on a title are made against the OWNER of the property, and unless you have an OWNER'S policy, it will be your duty to assume the cost of defending your title in order to protect yourself and the holder of your mortgage.
4. Even though the bank, (mortgagee) has a title policy, you, as owner of the property, have no protection without an OWNER'S policy, if you wish to sell or refinance your home if the new purchaser or lender claims that your title is defective.

Question: What protection is guaranteed by such a policy?

Answer:
1. The opinion of the company that your title is valid and marketable.
2. An indemnity or guarantee by said company backing up that opinion to protect you and those who succeed to your interest by operation of law, against loss or damage.

Question: Does the buyer have to pay more than one premium?

Answer: No. For the cost of one premium, protection is afforded as long as you own your home. And without further premium your heirs or those to whom you leave your property will receive the same protection.

It should also be noted that the cost of an OWNER'S policy is comparatively small, if ordered at the same time that the bank obtains its policy. The reason being that only one search of title is required.

TITLE ENCUMBRANCES: After requesting a title search, an inspection should always be made of the property. While it is a rule of law that ownership of real estate is established by the recording of a deed, such rule will not apply to the case of tenants in possession of the property, who have previously bought such property and failed to record the deed.

Question: John Jones duly executes and delivers a deed of his property to Sam Brown. Jones induces Brown not to record his deed for at least ten days. (Jones is not a tenant, and is not in possession). Jones immediately conveys the same property to Robert Smith, (who has no knowledge of the prior sale to Brown,) and Smith promptly records his deed in the County Clerk's office. In the meantime, the seller, John Jones disappears and cannot be traced. Upon discovering these facts, Sam Brown sues to set aside the second sale of the property to Smith, on the ground that his deed bore an earlier date, and was delivered 10 days prior to the sale to Smith. What should be the Court's decision.

Answer: Unfortunately for BROWN, he cannot recover. His failure to record his deed promptly has caused this situation. He has been tricked by a dishonest seller. When Smith bought the property, the record did not show any deed recorded in the name of BROWN, therefor, he received a title clear of BROWN'S claims. BROWN'S only remedy would be in the nature of criminal proceedings against the missing seller, alleging larceny.

Question: BROWN forges a deed to real property, and claiming to be the owner, sells such property to Smith. Smith thereafter sells the property to JONES. At this point, the true owner of the property, X, brings an action to eject SMITH from possession of the property.

JONES defends against this action, stating that when he purchased this property, he had promptly recorded the deed. What are the rights of the parties?

Answer: X is still the rightful owner. A purchaser of stolen goods or in this case, of real property, is not considered a bonda fide purchaser. A purchaser of real property who receives a forged deed does not obtain title to the property, and such transfer is null and void . . .

The report on the condition of the title should be obtained well in advance of the closing date, in order that the buyer may determine that the obligations assumed by him will not be greater than those provided for in the contract. There are very few parcels of real property which are not burdened by various encumbrances. Their most common form are as follows:
1. Mortgages
2. Taxes
3. Water Charges; Sewer Charges
4. Local assessments
5. Judgements recorded against the name of the owner.
6. Tenancies

7. Mechanic's liens for labor or materials supplied to the owner's building.
8. Court actions pending against the owner, involving a lien. (Lis Pendens)
9. Encroachments—Owner's building may overlap the adjoining property.
10. Easements—Rights given by present or previous owners to third parties for a right of way; rights to erect poles; string overhead wires or cables; rights to display advertising signs.
11. Restrictions—The owners, past and present, have been limited in the use of the use of the property, by restrictions placed in prior deeds or recorded written agreements between previous owners, such as, use for only specified purposes, (a one family house); type of construction; (only brick); limitation as to size of house in relation to the plot; certain set-backs from the building line.
12. Violations—Written notices from State or municipal officers, addressed to the owners, lessees or occupants of real estate, requiring compliance with existing laws respecting these properties.

ENCUMBRANCES NOT MENTIONED IN CONTRACT: When a contract is entered into for the purchase of real property, and no reference is made therein to encumbrances, the owner is bound to transfer a title, free and clar of any and all encumbrances. In order for the seller to convey title, the contract must specifically state the existence of all encumbrances, leaving it up to the purchaser, whether to accept or reject any of them. For example, if there is a tenant in possession, such tenancy must be stated in the contract. Even though the buyer had knowledge of such tenancy, the failure to mention it in the contract, will be sufficient excuse for the buyer to insist upon a completely vacant house at the time of closing of title.

Encumbrances such as mortgages, tax liens or judgements may be removed or satisfied by the seller prior to closing, by merely paying the amount due, and submitting such proof of payment to the buyer. On the other hand, it may be impossible to remove such encumbrances as encroachments, easements, restrictive covenants, leases, because in such instances the consent of persons holding these rights must be obtained in the form of written consent. If persons holding such rights refuse to release them; are out of town or otherwise unavailable, the owner cannot convey a marketable title.

Question: What precautions should a seller observe, when he desires to sell his property, against which there are a number of encumbrances?

Answer: The owner should insist on a provision in the contract, that the buyer agrees to purchase the property subject to certain stated encumbrances. For example:

1. Subject to the encroachment of the seller's premises of 3 inches on the property immediately adjoining the easterly boundary.
2. Subject to restrictions contained in former deeds requiring all buildings on the property herein conveyed to be built of brick; for one family use only; to cost not less than $15,000, and to be set back at least 15 feet from the building line.
3. Subject to an easement granted to the Telephone Company, permitting them to maintain overhead wires.
4. Subject to a lease of the ground floor premises, now held by William Smith, expiring ...., 19 ..... Said lease has been presented to the purchaser for his inspection.
5. Subject to a first mortgage in the sum of $25,000, which is now a first lien on the premises, bearing interest at the rate of 8 per cent; payable quarterly.

LIS PENDENS: A court action which has been started against an owner of real property, is a public warning that the rights of the owner are being attacked. The purpose of such notice, called a lis pendens, is to prevent the transfer of the full legal title. If a purchaser buys property, after the date of the filing of this notice, he does so subject to the rights of the parties involved in the litigation. In all such cases, the purchaser has bought a doubtful title, and if the suit is lost by the seller, the purchaser is also bound by any judgement.

Question: John Jones contracts to sell his property to Smith on Feb. 1, title closing to take place on March 15. However, on Feb. 2, Brown, a plumber, files an action against the owner, Jones, on the ground that he has not been paid his bill for completing extensive installations on Jones' house. At the closing of title, Smith asks for a definition of his rights.

Answer: A lis pendens can be removed only by a court order. If a judgement is entered against Jones, it becomes a lien against him and future owners, including Smith. The seller may settle this litigation prior to the closing of title, and a written agreement filed in court consenting to the cancellation of the lis pendens. Smith, the purchaser, should insist, upon the closing of title, if the action is still pending that the seller, Jones, deposit in escrow, with a stakeholder, an amount sufficient, to pay any judgment plus costs, secured by the plumber. Note: A Lis Pendens may be filed against an owner's property, only where the lawsuit involves the property, such as an action to foreclose a mortgage; recovery of a deposit, where owner has defaulted under the terms of his contract; the collection of a judgement against the owner; foreclosure of a mechanics lien, such as painters, plumbers, contractors.

In this connection, attempts have been made by real estate brokers to file a Lis Pendens, based on brokerage commissions claimed to be due, thereby seeking to prevent the passage of title. The courts, however invariably, refuse to permit a Lis Pendens to be filed in such actions. The broker's claim for commission must first be reduced to judgment, and filed against the owners property. If such judgement is filed after the sale of the property to the buyer, there is then no obligation on the part of the purchaser to pay such an outstanding claim.

Deeds

The written instrument conveying the title to the property is called a deed. In order to be effective as a legal document, this deed must be delivered and accepted by the purchaser.

Most contracts contain the following clause with respect to the deed to be delivered at the time of the closing of title.

"The deed shall be the usual .... deed in proper statutory form for record and shall be duly executed, acknowledged by the seller, so as to convey to the Purchaser the fee simple of the said premises, free from all encumbrances, except as herein stated."

Unless the purchaser obtains a stipulation of the kind of deed that he desires in such clause, upon the closing of title he will be required to accept a Bargain and Sale Deed, with the consequent possible loss of future rights.

Although purchasers frequently request that title be conveyed to them by a Full Covenant and Warranty Deed, because the seller in such a deed makes several important guaranties to the buyer, it is becoming increasingly difficult to obtain them, because sellers do not wish to assume any future obligations after the sale of the property.

MEANING OF FULL COVENANT WARRANTIES: The first covenant is the seller's guaranty of ownership, and a subsequent failure of title on his part will cause him to be liable in damages to the purchaser.

The second covenant guaranteeing quiet enjoyment means that the purchaser must remain in quiet possession, and that any attack on the purchaser's title, constitutes a breach of the seller's contract.

The third covenant entitles the purchaser a title free from all encumbrances, except those specifically excluded.

The fourth covenant providing for "further assurance" means that, if after the transfer of title, it becomes necessary for the buyer to obtain additional instruments affecting the title from the seller, the seller has agreed to procure such further proof of title.

The fifth covenant guarantees absolute title to the property, whenever attacked by any third party. If a judgement affecting the title is obtained, the buyer may have recourse under this judgment against the seller, for any damages sustained.

The choice between these two deeds is obvious, but the buyer should always be mindful of the fact that a full covenant and warranty deed provides little protection unless the seller has a clear title. While a purchaser may sue a seller under the warranties in a Full Covenant and Warranty, the question of the seller's financial responsibility and availability for suit must be considered.

Proper precautions require that the purchaser in all cases, regardless of the type of deed offered, should obtain a policy of title insurance. Under this form of property insurance, the company guarantees an owner of property against any loss through a defect in title.

The following problem illustrates the foregoing discussion:

Question: Jones dies, leaving no will and is survived by three sons. One of these sons has been unheard from for many years. Thereafter, the two remaining sons sell the property to Brown, representing that they are the only two surviving heirs of Jones.

Brown now sells the property to Daniel by means of a Full Covenant and Warranty Deed. Ten years later the missing son returns, and claims a one-third interest in the property. Daniel notifies Brown of this claim, and demands that this defect in the title be cleared. What are the rights of the parties?

Answer: The third son has an interest in the property which must be satisfied. Daniel, the present owner is fortunate in having received a Full Covenant and Warranty Deed, and can compel his seller, (Brown) to reimburse him under the warranties.

Question: Would the result be different, if in the preceding question, Daniel had received a Bargain and Sale Deed?

Answer: Yes. In such a case the loss would fall upon

Daniel, because under such a deed, the purchaser receives only the title owned by the seller, which at all times consisted of no more than a two-thirds interest in the property.

Contract Defaults by Seller or Buyer

If either the seller or buyer fail or refuse to perform their contract obligations, an action may be instituted against the defaulting party, called an action for Specific Performance.

In such a proceeding, the court may direct the seller to convey the property, under penalty of being held in contempt of court, or compel a defaulting buyer to proceed likewise.

However, if after default, a seller has conveyed such property to an innocent third person, such a proceeding will not be effective. In such a case, a buyer would be entitled to the return of his deposit, the reasonable cost of examination of the title, and in addition provable money damages.

A seller may waive such a suit against a defaulting buyer, and instead re-sell his property to a third party. If the subsequent sale to this third party results in a lower price, than originally called for in the defaulted contract, the seller may sue for such difference.

In cases where the seller has a defective title, the courts will not grant him permission to sue and recover in Specific Performance, because if the buyer loses this suit, he is entitled to a marketable title.

Buyer and Sellers Check List

The following check list presents a clue to most problems facing buyers and sellers, and a careful reading is suggested in order to avoid the most common pitfalls found in realty contracts.

1. Legal capacity of the contracting parties. (Sane Adults)
2. Proper Description.
3. Nature of Deed (Full Covenant—Bargain and Sale.

4—Ownership of Personal Property in House.
5—Nature of the mortgage obligation—Grace clauses, prepayment privileges.
6—Rate of amortization and amount of interest.
7—Adjustments and credits on closing of title.
8—Existing tenancies
9—Guaranty of Possession
10—Is "time to be of the essence"?
12—Date when existing mortgage must be paid
13—Assessments
14—Condemnation proceedings
15—Changes in Zoning
16—Nature of restrictions governing property use
17—Easements showing rights of third persons
18—Encroachments on adjoining property
19—Certificate of Occupancy
20—Down payment held in Escrow
21—Assignment of Builder's guaranties, (Roof, Cellar, etc.)
22—Up to-date Survey
23—Payment of Taxes and Fuel Bills by Seller
24—Adequate insurance
25—Violations, Noted and Unnoted in Public records.

Final Closing Preparations

1—The *PURCHASER* should compare the seller's deed with the description in the contract.
2—Prepare certified check for an approximate amount and extra cash for final adjustments.
3—Obtain letter of ownership in case of tenancies.
4—If mortgage has been reduced by seller, obtain a certificate of such reduction from owner and mortgagee.
1—The *SELLER* should bring with him all insurance policies.
2—Produce all paid tax, water, fuel, assessment bills.
3—Latest readings of utility meter readings, eg. gas, electric, telephone.
4—Bill of Sale covering personal property, eg. refrigerators, gas ranges.

Chapter 5

POINTERS FOR BROKERS

It is obvious that an owner can sell his own property and save a commission, and that at times, a buyer can make his own independent search for an owner thinking he is saving a commission, thus lessening the purchase price.

Likewise, a man can act as his own lawyer, or extract an aching tooth or repair his own car. But experience has taught buyers and sellers that the wisest economy is to go to the market place, the real estate brokers office.

The well-equipped broker's office can offer valuable advice regarding the characteristics of the neighborhood in question: Nature of population, neighborhood conditions; value ranges; type of improvements; projected zoning changes; aid to the seller in eliminating undesirable prospects; arranging convenient inspection hours, and finally conducting all preliminary negotiations.

Commissions

The commissions are usually paid by the seller. A buyer may not be held liable for commissions unless he has made a definite commitment to that effect.

The contract of employment of a broker may be oral or in writing. If the parties stipulate that a certain fee is to be paid, they are bound by their agreement. If the work of the broker has been completed, the court may not question the reasonableness of the fee. However, if no fee has been set, the court will fix an amount to which the broker is entitled, it being customary in such cases, to use the rates established by the local real estate boards.

Sellers must be mindful of the fact that, in the absence of a written agreement of employment, a broker has earned his commission when he has produced a buyer ready, able and willing to meet the seller's terms and price.

Question: Jones, a seller, orally engages Brown, a broker, to sell his house for $15,000. all cash. Brown produces a buyer who is ready, willing and able to consummate this deal, but Jones advises the broker that he has changed his mind about selling the property, because he has been unable to find other suitable living quarters. What are the rights of the parties?

Anwser: The broker is entitled to recover a commission. An owner may not use the services of a broker in order to investigate the value of his property without liability therefor. If the seller had required the broker, at the time of employment, to waive a commission in such a change of heart situation, the seller would then not be bound. (Note: In some states a written authorization of employment is required from the seller.)

Question: In the foregoing problem, may the purchaser produced by the broker, compel the seller to transfer title to him, by means of a Specific Performance action?

Answer: No. As between a seller and the buyer, no rights under law can be established, unless and until the parties have entered into a valid written legal contract.

VOLUNTEERS: Unless the broker has been employed by the seller, he has no legal claim to a commission. A person who inquires of an owner the asking price of his property, even though he is a broker, is not entitled to a commission. Even though a buyer is produced at the same or even better terms, an owner may not be enticed into paying a commission against his will. The broker must offer his services in such capacity, and be accepted by the owner.

CONFLICTING BROKERAGE CLAIMS: An owner may list his property for sale with as many brokers as he chooses. If an owner has employed a broker by means of a carefully drawn contract, there can usually be no disputes.

However, in the great majority of cases there is no such

formal agreement made. The request to the brokers may be oral, or a brief listing by letter, which omits to state many of the necessary terms concerning the sale. In such cases, the law presumes that when any one of these brokers has found an acceptable purchaser, the authority of all other brokers is automatically revoked. No notice of revocation to the other brokers need be given, in case of such prior sale by the other broker. Such rule of law is necessary for the protection of property owners, who might otherwise incur liability for two or more commissions.

BROKER ACTING FOR BOTH PARTIES: Since the financial situation of the buyer and seller are diametrically opposed to each other, it is ordinarily improper for a broker to represent and take commissions from both parties to the transaction, unless both parties are fully informed and consent to such arrangement.

The rule of law which prohibits such divided loyalty is obvious. A broker's employer has the right to expect that the broker will try to get the maximum price for his property. By failing to disclose his conflicting interests, the broker is perpetrating a fraud upon both parties, and if these facts are discovered, the broker forfeits all rights to compensation from either party.

However, if both parties consent and know all the facts, no wrong has been committed, and the broker may collect full commissions from each party, if each has agreed to pay him.

Exclusive Agreements of Employment

Question: John Brown, a broker, has been employed to procure a purchaser for a two family house; thereafter the broker is notified that his employment has been terminated; later the owner sells the same property himself. Is Brown entitled to a commission under these facts?

Answer: No. An owner may terminate the broker's agency, if done in good faith, even where the broker has expended money in advertising or has shown the property to countless prospects. Unless such sale was made to a client procured by the broker, the owner is within his rights in canceling such agency.

The broker should have protected his investment of time and money by obtaining from the owner either an "exclusive *Agency* of sale", or an "exclusive *Right of Sale*" for a definite period, permitting him ample time to negotiate for prospective purchasers.

EXCLUSIVE AGENCY: Unless a broker's employment is stated to be exclusive, any other broker may be entitled to a commission upon producing a purchaser, satisfactory to the seller. Where a non-exclusive agency has been given to a broker, it should be quite clear that the seller himself may still negotiate the sale of his property without the broker's aid, and such sale automatically terminates the agency of all non-exclusive brokers.

However, in the case of an "exclusive agency" the situation changes. The courts generally hold that a contract which states merely that the broker has an "exclusive agency" to sell certain property, does not make the seller liable to the broker, if the seller himself makes a sale without the intervention or aid of any broker within the time period of the exclusive agency. The theory of law applied is that the owner has merely promised to employ no other brokers, but has not waived the right to make a sale himself.

EXCLUSIVE RIGHT: Where, however, the seller has granted an exclusive *right*, such a clause is generally interpreted to cover even sales by the owner himself. If, after making such an exclusive *right* contract with the broker, the owner, nevertheless, sells the property himself, he remains liable for a commission. The same rule would apply even where a third broker effected the sale, during the period of the exclusive right. Depending on the situation as affecting the seller's or the broker's position, care should be exercised as to the nature and language of the exclusive agreement. (See form below.)

EXCLUSIVE AGENCY FORM

I hereby grant to John Jones, a licensed real estate broker, the (Exclusive Agency) (Exclusive Right) to sell my property located at No. 1 Broadway, New York, N. Y. under the following terms and conditions:

Price — $75,000.
Cash — $15,000.

Subject to a mortgage now existing on these premises, in the amount of $60,000. bearing interest at 6 per cent, due in 8 years.

As and for your compensation for selling my premises, the seller hereby agrees to pay the sum of one thousand ($1,000.) dollars. The seller further agrees that the broker herein will have the (Exclusive Agency) (Exclusive Right) for a period of 30 days from the date hereof.

The broker hereby agrees to exert all reasonable efforts and with due diligence to effect such sale.

Dated, ...

....
Seller

....
Broker

Question: If an owner uses information supplied to him by the broker and, he himself sold the property to the broker's client, after waiting for the termination of the exclusive, would the broker be deprived of his commission?

Answer: No. In such a situation, the law will imply bad faith on the part of the owner, and will presume that the owner consented to extend the time of the exclusive by accepting the prior customer and concluding the sale with him.

(Note: Brokers desirous of avoiding such situations frequently insert the following clause in their exclusive agreements.)

"In the event that any customer produced by the broker herein, purchases the property within 60 days after the termination of this exclusive agreement, the seller shall be liable to such broker for a brokerage commission."

NAMING OF BROKER IN CONTRACT: Most contracts of sale contain the following clause; "The seller and buyer agree that .... brought about this sale and the Seller agrees to pay the broker's commission."

While it seems that such clause is designed solely to protect the broker, experience has shown that such clause actually affords the seller an added degree of protection against unfounded commission claims. The seller should seek to limit his liability, if he has dealt with several brokers, and should therefor obtain the signature of the buyer to this clause, so that, in effect, the buyer will not, if he should so desire, later state, that a third broker had negotiated this sale in his behalf.

In order to insure a greater degree of safety to the seller in such situations, where the possibility of conflicting commission claims are present, the following Purchaser's Agreement is suggested:

PURCHASER'S AGREEMENT

"The Purchaser warrants to the Seller that this sale was brought about by .... broker; that all negotiations were handled by said broker; that no other broker assisted in this sale.

The Purchaser agrees that should any claim for broker's commission be made by any other broker, because of any acts or dealings on the part of the Purchaser, the Purchaser agrees to hold the Seller free and harmless from any liability."

The Broker's Authority

The power of a broker is ordinarily limited to the finding of a purchaser to the property. He has no right to enter into or sign a binding contract, unless such authority is expressly conferred in writing. In most sections of the country, the real estate broker also engages in property management, involving collection of rents, making of repairs and negotiation of leases.

In addition, he may make appraisals; auction real property and negotiate mortgage loans for property owners; as a sideline, he is often a licensed insurance broker and is thus able to place the various types of insurance coverages needed by the home owner.

DUTIES OF A BROKER TO THE SELLER: The broker owes his client the highest fidelity with respect to any and all transactions involving the sale of the property. He is bound by good faith to use all diligent means to effect a transfer of the property. He must not exceed the scope of his authority, and may not represent conflicting interests. He may not wilfully represent or conceal vital information, benefitting the seller. Failing in such duties, the broker is liable to the forfeit of any commission.

DUTY OF THE SELLER TO THE BROKER: The seller may not deliberately prevent the completion of the broker's negotiations by discharging him just prior to the signing of contract; nor may the seller avoid liability for commissions, where it can be shown that he and the prospective purchaser conspired to deprive the broker of his rightful compensation. In such latter case, the purchaser, too, may be liable in damages to the broker.

Bad faith on the part of the seller is not one of the risks of failure assumed by a broker.

DEAL FAILING DUE TO FAULT OF PRINCIPAL: Generally speaking, if the broker produces a purchaser who is ready, willing and financially able to buy on the terms offered by the owner, and the latter then arbitrarily or capriciously refuses to enter into a contract with the purchaser;

or if the owner attempts to insert new terms and conditions, not previously stipulated, as a result of which the purchaser refuses to sign the contract, the owner, under both of these situations, is liable for the broker's commission. This result follows logically from the well established legal principle that one party to a brokerage contract cannot plead the other party's non-performance as a defense, if he himself has prevented that other party from performing.

Brokers and Secret Profits

Closely related to the rule of law which prohibits a broker from secretly accepting an inconsistent employment (*e.g.* dual commissions from buyer and seller), is another rule which requires a broker to disclose any personal interest he may have in the transaction.

Suppose a broker with whom property is listed desires to buy the property himself, and procures a dummy to make an offer, which is accepted by the owner, and the deal is closed. Later, the seller learns that the broker himself was the real purchaser. In such a case, the seller has a right to rescind this transaction; obtain a reconveyance of title, and also to recover any commissions he has paid to the broker.

If the broker has resold this property to an innocent third party, for a valuable consideration, the seller of course cannot reclaim this property. He can, however, compel the broker to account for any profits he might have received.

In such cases, it makes no difference that the broker can show to the court that the seller was not injured by the deception. The courts invariably rule that such a conflict of interest, gives the seller an absolute right to refuse to perform the contract, or to revoke it if it has been completed, regardless of the intrinsic fairness of the price obtained by the seller.

It must be carefully noted, however, that a seller must act promptly upon discovering the fraud. He cannot wait to see whether the property will rise in value, before electing to sue. If he delays unreasonably, after obtaining the facts, he will be deemed to have affirmed the contract, and his right to recission will be barred. A leading decision on this subject states,

"The disclosure of the broker's interest in the purchase of property, must be definite and unequivocal, and to be effective, where dual interests are involved, such disclosure must lay bare the truth, without ambiguity or reservation, in all its stark significance."

Question: May a broker buy property listed with him for sale, if he acted openly in the transaction, and has fully and fairly revealed all pertinent facts to the seller regarding the identity of the buyer?

Answer: Yes.

General Commission Rules

It is well established that a broker is not entitled to commissions for unsuccessful efforts. The risk or failure is wholly assumed by him. His reward comes only with his success in producing an acceptable buyer. He may expend time and money with the highest devotion to the interest of the seller, yet if he does not effect a bargain, or if his agency is terminated fairly and in good faith by the seller, he gains no right to commissions. He may even have planted the seed in the mind of the purchaser; yet if he abandons the deal, or suspends the continuity of his negotiations, another broker may reap the harvest of the first broker's spadework.

Question: At what point in the negotiations is the broker entitled to his commission?

Answer: When he has produced a buyer ready, able and willing to sign a contract of purchase. The broker must prove that he has been authorized to represent the employer. Unless the broker at the time of employment agreed to defer his commission, he is entitled to it at the signing of the contract, and need not wait for the closing of title.

Question: In addition to showing authorization and acting as the "procuring cause" in the sale, what other condition must usually be met by the broker in his claim for a commission?

Answer: In most of our states, a necessary prerequisite to claiming a commission is the requirement that the broker and any salesmen who might have assisted him in the negotiations, are duly qualified to act as such agents by having obtained a license.

Question: What is required of an applicant, in order that he may qualify for a real estate broker's license?

Answer: The State of New York, a pioneer in license law requirements, and a model for most states in this respect, sets the following standards:

An applicant must be a citizen of good moral character; be familiar with the English language; have a good general understanding of the law of contracts, deeds, leases, mortgages, and understand the obligations existing between principal and broker. The applicant must also have been licensed as a real estate salesman for a period of not less than two years under the supervision of a broker, or had the equivalent experience as a real estate operator for the same period. Applicants who are salesmen, may substitute a course in a recognized school, for the second year of apprenticeship. Finally, the aspirant must pass a comprehensive written examination.

Question: What are the grounds for the suspension or revocation of a broker's license?

Answer:

1—A material misstatement in the application (*e.g.* concealing a crime).
2—Fraudulent dealings.
3—Ethical misconduct.
4—Incompetency in his dealings.
5—Misleading advertising.
6—General untrustworthiness.

Rules of Conduct

The following comprehensive regulations are presently in effect in the State of New York, and are deemed quite inclusive in defining and limiting the sphere of a broker's activities.

1—A real estate broker shall not commingle the money or other property of his principal with his own.

2—A real estate broker shall, within a reasonable time, render an account to his client, and remit to him, any monies collected and unexpended for his account.

3—When acting as an agent in the management of property, a real estate broker shall not accept any rebate on expenditures made for his client, without the latter's full knowledge and consent.

4—A broker shall not directly or indirectly buy for himself property listed with him, nor shall he acquire any interest therein without making his true position clearly known to the listing owner.

5—Before a broker buys property for a client, in the ownership of which the broker has a financial interest, he shall disclose such fact.

6—Before a broker sells property in which he owns an interest, he shall make such interest known to the purchaser.

7—A broker shall not receive compensation from more than one party, except with the full knowledge and consent of all parties.

8—No broker shall negotiate directly with an owner or lessor, if he knows that such parties, have an existing written contract granting an exclusive authority with another broker.

9—No broker shall induce any party to a contract to break such contract, for the purpose of substituting a new contract with another principal.

10—A broker shall never offer a property for sale or lease without the authorization of the owner.

11—A broker shall immediately deliver a duplicate original of any document to any person signing the same, where such instrument has been prepared by the broker, and which relates to the employment of the broker, or to the sale, lease or exchange of real property in which the broker may participate.

12—A broker may not accept the services of any employee of another broker without the knowledge and consent of such other broker.

13—No sign shall ever be placed on any property (For Sale—For Rent) without the consent of the owner.

14—A real estate salesman shall, upon termination of his employment, forthwith turn over to his broker all listings obtained by him, while so employed.

15—No broker shall be a party to an exclusive listing contract which shall contain an automatic continuation of the period of such listing beyond the fixed termination date set forth therein.

Broker's Opinions and Representations

Unauthorized and misleading statements made by a broker will result in a denial of his claim to commissions and justification on the part of the purchaser in refusing to complete the deal. A misstatement regarding a material matter, such as size of the lot; nature of a tenancy; rent payable; amount of existing mortgage and its terms are examples.

However, praising a property to the skies, or listing its potentialities for future value, is merely selling talk, and will not justify a purchaser in rescinding the contract, if the broker's and buyers hopes are not realized.

Termination of a Broker's Authority

The employment of a broker may be terminated under the following conditions.
(a) By mutual consent
(b) Notice of such termination, if made in good faith
(c) Prior sale by another broker
(d) Destruction of the property (by fire or other casualty) before contract signing
(e) Death of either party
(f) Insanity of either party
(g) Bankruptcy
(h) Failure to produce a customer after the lapse of a reasonable time

Brokers and Salesmen

Employees of a broker are bound by the same restrictions under the licensing laws. It is the duty of the broker to exercise the closest supervision of his salesman's activities, and to guard against his excess zeal at times, in order to earn a commission. A salesman may not advertise in his own name, but must conduct all his negotiations in the name of his principal.

Many weaknesses in the broker and salesman relationship arises out of the failure in most cases to enter into a written contract defining the rights of the parties. No matter how long or short the agreement, it should be in writing, and should specify, for example, the rates of compensation; procedure regarding listings; manner or method of closing sales; disposition of deposits; and finally, after termination of employment, a possible restriction of the salesman's future place of business.

Question: John Smith, a salesman employed by Brown, a broker, has effected a sale. Smith demands his commission on behalf of his employer, and the seller refuses to pay. Smith's employer, Brown, who is friendly with the seller, refuses to be involved in any law suit. Smith thereupon sues the seller in his own name. What disposition should be made?

Answer: A salesman may not ordinarily sue a seller. Such right is reserved only to the broker. However, the salesman is not without remedy. He may, if he desires, sue the broker for damages, in an amount equivalent to the commissions he might have earned.

Question: Jones, a broker, is employed by a wife to sell her one-family house. Jones obtains a purchaser who is ready, willing and able to meet the terms proposed in the wife's listing. Thereafter, the husband refuses to sign the contract, and the deal collapses. Is the broker entitled to any commission?

Answer: Yes. The broker has fully performed. The wife by employing the broker, has apparently held herself forth as having authority to negotiate the sale, and will be therefore held liable.

Chapter 6

THE LANDLORD AND TENANT RELATIONSHIP

The relationship is founded upon a contract between the parties, whereby the landlord agrees to give possession of certain property in return for the payment of rent.

Like most real estate contracts, this agreement, called a lease, must be in writing, except where the period of leasing is less than one year.

The Essentials of a Valid Lease

1. Competent Parties (Sane Adults);
2. Agreement between the Landlord (Lessor) and Tenant (Lessee) accepting lease obligations;
3. A reasonably definite description of the premises;
4. The term (duration) of the agreement;
5. Amount of rent payable, and method of payment; (Monthly, weekly, etc.)
6. Delivery and acceptance of the lease;
7. If the term is for more than one year, it must be in writing and signed.

Under the terms of a lease, the parties may agree to any terms and conditions, except the carrying out of some illegal act.

RENT CONTROL LIMITATIONS: Although this legislation is temporary in character, nevertheless those tenants covered under rent control leases, are subject to the paramount controls exercised by local governments.

Eviction of tenants under such leases may not be had, irrespective of the terms of the original lease, unless:

1. The property is sold in good faith and occupied by the new owner.
2. Complete conversion of the property; (Major alterations).

3. Failure to pay rent or material breach of lease terms (e.g. using premises for immoral purpose).

The main purpose of rent controls is to protect tenants against undue increases in rent, permitting adjustment to the landlord in cases of hardship or where substantial major improvements have been installed.

Question: Jones is about to purchase a two family house. The premises are subject to rent control. What precautions should Jones, the buyer take, with regard to an existing tenancy

Answer: The purchaser should require that the contract should include a representation that the rental received by the seller is not in excess of the maximum rentals permitted by the local rent regulations; that the seller has complied with all such regulations. The purchaser should require a copy of all reports filed regarding such rentals; copies of notices regarding rent increases mailed to such tenant; and finally, a representation from the landlord that there are no preceedings pending by the present tenant for a reduction in rent.

POSSESSION BEFORE TITLE: In a number of instances, a sales transaction may grant the buyer the right to take possession before the closing of title. However, such a situation may cause a seller substantial injustice.

In the event of discovering of a flaw in the seller's title, or the buyer is unable to complete adequate financing, considerable expense and a prolonged legal proceeding might be required to remove the purchaser. In some cases, the buyer, in anticipation of a clear title has started remodeling the premises; painting or redecorating, and then stops such work, leaving the owner with the expense of either finishing the job, or restoring the house to its previous original condition.

In certain cases, where there has been an advantageous sale, the seller may take a calculated risk and allow possession before title passes. But in the greatest majority of cases, the prudent seller will refuse, and instead exert every possible pressure to remove flaws in the title, or obtain adequate financing, and remove any other valid objections before closing of title.

However, where a possession is permitted before closing, the seller should observe the following precautions.

1. The seller should obtain an agreement from the buyer, that the relationship between the parties is that of landlord and tenant, until the tenant receives his deed. In such a case, the owner, if the need arises, will have less legal difficulty and expense in removing the purchaser.
2. The tenant (purchaser) should be required to pay a certain stipulated amount of rent monthly, until completion of the sales transaction.
3. The seller and buyer may agree that the deed will be held in escrow, and delivered when purchaser has completed his bargain.

Question: Jones, the owner of a two family house, verbally agreed to rent one of his apartments to Brown for a period of three years, at a rental of $400. per month. Later, Jones, the owner receives an offer of $550. per month for the same apartment from Smith. Jones informs Brown that unless he agrees to match this offer of $550, he would have to vacate the premises. Brown refuses to pay the increase or to move, on the ground that he holds a lease which does not expire for a period of about two years. After giving Brown notice of his intention to terminate the lease, the landlord commences a dispossess (summary) proceeding to oust Brown. What are the tenant's rights?

Answer: (The solution of this problem and the further discussions in this chapter presuppose the absence of rent control.) A verbal agreement to lease property for more than one year is unenforceable, and therefore, the tenant will be compelled to remove from the premises as a hold-over. Under, these facts, the tenancy expired when he failed to move upon the expiration of the notice served on him by the landlord to vacate.

EXECUTION AND DELIVERY OF A LEASE: It is a common practice for a tenant to execute a lease in duplicate, and in many cases, deliver both copies to an agent or representative of the landlord, and then wait for the fully executed signed copy to be returned with the landlord's signature.

It must be understood by tenants, that prior to the return of the signed landlord's copy of the lease, the tenant's signing is no more than an *offer* to lease. The proper practise from the tenant's viewpoint is to obtain a simultaneous exchange of signed leases, or, if this is not possible, the tenant's lease which is being transmitted to the landlord, should be accompanied by a letter, expressly stating that the delivery of the tenant's lease has no legal effect, unless he receives the landlord's fully executed signed copy within a specified time limit. The purpose of such letter being to prevent undue delay and stalling tactics on the part of a landlord unsure of his bargain.

NEGOTIATION OF LEASES: The ordinary residential lease is generally unaccompanied by the formalities attending the purchase and sale of a home. The parties usually rely on the inspection of the premises; location; rent payable; nature of tenant's references and credit standing, and invariably, sign a lease form containing many printed provisions, containing clauses little understood nor wanted, if fully explained. In most cases, the tenant does not seek legal advice, but feels that, at most, his tenancy, will last but one or two years, and he will remove at expiration if his lease obligations become too onerous.

A word as to these printed forms is in order. While customarily used, they generally offer pitfalls both to the landlord and to the tenant. There is nothing objectionable to a reasonable request from a tenant for a change in the printed form lease, and a similar rule applies to the landlord. For example, let us take the question of the renewal of a lease.

Question: Is a tenant entitled to a renewal of his lease without an express written agreement to that effect.

Answer: No.

Question: A landlord has agreed in the lease to grant his tenant the right to renewal of his lease under the same terms and conditions of the previous lease. Is the tenant bound to renew?

Answer: Such an obligation on the part of the landlord's part, without a definite acceptance by the tenant, constitutes no more than an option, which may or not be exercised by the tenant.

Question: A tenant has been granted the right to renew his lease. However, at the time of exercising such renewal, he is in default in payment of rent and has committed other breaches of his lease. Is the tenant still entitled to demand the privilege granted of a renewal

Answer: Yes. The landlord might have failed to require that the tenant must be in good standing under his lease, at the time a renewal request is made. The use of the following clause in a lease is suggested in such instances:

> "The Landlord covenants and agrees that if the Tenant shall, during the whole of the term of his lease, well and faithfully keep and perform the lease obligations on his part, the Landlord will, at the expiration of said lease, grant a new lease to Tenant under the same terms and conditions of the previous lease."

THE LEASED PREMISES: The lease should describe with particularity the premises granted. If a tenant has or expects the right to use personal property on the premises, such right should be agreed upon. Use of a garden, porch, basement washing machines, garages for common purposes are examples.

TERM OF THE LEASE: If, on execution of the lease, as sometimes happens, the premises are occupied by a third person, important considerations arise as to the right of possession by the new tenant. The rules are in conflict at this point. Under the so-called English Rule, applicable in many states, the landlord is not bound to give the tenant actual possession.

Under the "American Rule" as applicable in New York and other states, the landlord is bound to give a new tenant only the "right" to possession. It will be seen, therefore, that the parties to a lease should make their own rule by agreement.

The parties should agree, in effect, that if possession under lease is postponed, (due to third party occupancy, incompleted repairs, or otherwise) for an unreasonable delay, or a specified period, rent will not be payable during such period, and that the tenant will not be liable for any further rent and is entitled to rescission of the lease agreement.

RENT: Unless the lease so provides, rent is not payable in advance. If a tenant has been given a rent concession, the question arises, whether such privilege can be claimed upon a renewal of the tenant's lease. In order to obtain a renewal of such concession, the language of the lease must be very explicit.

Question: Under the terms of his written lease, Jones is required to pay $300. rent monthly. Due to financial reverses, Jones obtains an oral agreement reducing the rent to $275 per month. Thereafter, the landlord changes his mind and demands the original $300. per month. May the tenant refuse?

Answer: No. There was no legal consideration for reducing the rent to $275. and the landlord may reinstate the original amount.

Question: A tenant negotiates for the rental of an

apartment, places a deposit and signs a lease for one year. Just prior to taking possession, the tenant advises the landlord that he has transferred his employment to a different state, and therefore, requests the return of his deposit. Is the landlord obligated to do so?

Answer: No. Not only may the landlord retain the deposit, but he may hold the tenant liable for the breach of his lease, up to a year's rent.

LANDLORD'S LIABILITY FOR REPAIRS: It is generally supposed that the duty to make repairs to leased premises falls upon the landlord. However, the reverse is the usual situation. In the absence of any provision in the lease, the duty of making repairs falls upon the tenant, except in the following situations:
1. Where the law imposes this duty on the landlord, as in the case of apartment houses;
2. Where the landlord has exclusive control of portions of the premises; stairways; halls, roof, yard, porch, etc.
3. A tenant is not liable for repairs which are major or structural in character; e.g. sagging floors, weakened foundation.

Unless the lease so requires, the landlord is not obligated to repaint or redecorate an apartment. As previously noted, in many jurisdictions, owners of multi-family houses are required by law periodically to redecorate the apartments of their tenants.

TERMINATION OF LEASES: A tenancy may end in the following situations.
1. Term has expired.
2. Actual eviction.
3. Constructive eviction.
4. Government condemnation of the Property.
5. Destruction of the Property by Fire or other Casualty.
6. Surrender and Acceptance by Landlord.
7. Foreclosure of Owner's (Landlord) Mortgage.

CONSTRUCTIVE EVICTION: Where the continued use of the premises becomes unbearable, because of acts or conditions permitted by the landlord, making further occupancy dangerous to the limb, life or health of the tenant, he may remove without any further liability for payment of rent for the unexpired term remaining. If a tenant claims such eviction, he must promptly vacate the premises. The acts causing such eviction must not have been caused by the tenant, otherwise, rent liability still remains.

FORECLOSURE OF A MORTGAGE: In many cases, the landlord's building is encumbered by a mortgage, at the time of the rental. If such mortgage is foreclosed, the tenant may lose his right to possession, unless he has made a prior agreement with the mortgagee, permitting him to remain as tenant, even after such a foreclosure.

ASSIGNMENT OF A LEASE: In order to transfer the obligations of a tenant, the agreement of the landlord for the substitution of a new tenant must be obtained. The original tenant who has received permission to assign his lease, is still responsible for any rent that might be due and unpaid by the substituted tenant, for the balance of the term of the unexpired lease.

AUTOMATIC RENEWAL CLAUSES: All clauses contained in a lease are binding on the parties, unless they are illegal or contrary to public policy. Another exception is found in many jurisdictions regarding the operation of the "automatic renewal clause." Provisions in leases that provide that the lease will be automatically renewed without further notice by landlord or tenant, on the same terms, unless either party gives the other party a notice to the contrary within a specified period while valid in some states, are not binding, for example, in New York. The law in such state requires that although such clause is incorporated in the lease, it is not binding, unless the landlord, at least 15 days and not more than thirty days previous to the time specified for the furnishing of such notice to him, shall give the tenant written notice, calling the attention of the tenant to the existence of such provision in the lease."

The purpose of such notice is to aid tenants avoid the penalty of forgetfulness, and thereby find themselves as hold-over tenants with a liability for a year's rent.

Question: May a tenant waive rights under a lease?

Answer: Yes. If such waiver is not against public policy. E.g. Right to a jury trial in dispossess proceedings.

Question: Jones, a tenant, in New York State, signs a lease, whereby he waives any obligation for the landlord to advise the tenant regarding the existence of the "automatic renewal clause." Is such waiver valid?

Answer: No. An attempt to effect such a waiver is against public policy, and will not be enforced by the courts.

SECURITY DEPOSITS: Money or securities deposited with a landlord by a tenant, to insure the faithful performance by tenant of the obligations assumed by him under the lease, are trust moneys and must be kept in a separate account. Such funds may not be used for the personal expenses of the landlord. If the landlord sells the house, he must transfer such security to the new owner and notify the tenant of such fact; or he must return such security deposit to the tenant; or may retain such deposit, and advise tenant. A failure to observe these rules, and a violation thereof, is a misdemeanor, making the landlord subject to a fine or imprisonment.

Question: Does a landlord have the right to enter your apartment without your permission?

Answer: Usually no. However, he may enter to demand payment of rent: in cases of emergency structural repairs to the building; or in compliance with orders issued by governmental authorities to remove violations.

Chapter 7
INSURING THE HOME

Insurance is a contract of indemnity, whereby the company, in return for the payment of a premium, agrees to protect the insured in case of loss.

In placing an order for property insurance, the aid of an experienced broker should always be enlisted. It is his function to survey your needs; thoroughly understand the risks involved; and place such coverages in financially sound companies, which are competitive in rates, and are prompt and fair in the settlement of losses.

Before a loss occurs, the property owner too often regards his insurance business as something to be given out as a favor. Policies are received and filed away without examination, despite the fact that the insured relies on such policy to rebuild his home, or safeguard him against a dangerous lawsuit. It is therefore essential to read carefully the policy provisions, and make proper inquiry concerning the various items covered, when in doubt as to their meaning.

After a fire, the insured usually thinks that he can collect enough money to buy a completely new house; new furniture or other new items to replace the damage, without regard to the depreciated value of his property. It must be understood that an insurance policy is a contract of indemnity and not a wager. The policy covering a building does not say, "If your house is burned we will give you a new one." It does state, however, that "if your house is damaged, we will pay what your actual loss is, but no profit."

Fire Insurance

Most states use the standard fire policy. Under this policy, damage caused by lightning is covered. Property owned by guests and servants of the owner is not covered, unless specific request and premium endorsement is issued.

Items not covered also include currency, deeds, promissory notes and securities. The reason for such exclusions is the problem of estimating the value of such property and the difficulty in checking the proof of such losses.

BUILDING PROPERTY COVERAGE: The policy covers all buildings on the property, additions and extensions; machinery and boilers; sidewalks; gates; signs; storm doors and permanent fixtures. Trees, plants, shrubbery flowers are not covered.

HOUSEHOLD CONTENTS COVERAGE: In case of loss, a requirement of the standard fire insurance policy is that the insured furnish a complete inventory of the damaged and undamaged property, setting forth in detail quantities of items; cost; actual cash value and amount of loss claimed.

It has been often said that the palest ink is better than the most retentive memory, and for this reason, in view of the inventory requirement, the policyholder should upon receipt of his policy, prepare such list in the event of possible claim. Such inventory should be subject to periodic review. Overall values change. Items are added, lost or otherwise disposed of. Keep such inventory in a safe place. Most insurance companies provide a printed inventory record to their insureds, which contain the following items covered, and blank spaces for insertion of values.

The list of household items covered are herewith presented:

> China, Furniture, Clocks, Closet Contents, Draperies, Lamps, Pictures, Rugs, Books, Musical Instruments, Phonograph and Records, Radio and Television, Silverware, Linens, Clothing, Electrical Appliances, Household Utensils, Refrigerators, Stove, Laundry Equipment, Power Tools and Supplies, Trunks and Contents, Heating Units, Food Supplies, Scales and Toilet Articles.

OBLIGATION ASSUMED BY THE INSURANCE COMPANY: While the insurance company agrees to pay in the event of loss, it must be borne in mind that a policy is void, and no recovery will be permitted, if the insured before or after a loss, has wilfully concealed or misrepresented any material fact or circumstance affecting the insurance. The fraudulent act or misrepresentation must be of a major character. Minor errors in proof of loss, for example, or exaggerated estimate of values will not ordinarily void a fire policy.

Question: Which perils or hazards are not covered by the standard fire insurance policy?

Answer: The company is not liable for loss covered by fire, whether caused directly or indirectly in the following circumstances:
> Enemy attack by armed forces; invasion; civil war; any acts of the insured himself which show neglect in saving and preserving his property when a loss occurs; nor is the company liable for theft from the premises.

Question: Is coverage afforded under a fire policy, when the loss is due solely to an explosion on the premises?

Answer: No. If, however, a fire occurs as the result of such explosion, payment shall be made for the fire damage caused by said explosion.

Question: May an insured obtain insurance protection for damage caused by an explosion?

Answer: Yes. Coverage may be added to the fire policy by endorsement for an additional charge.

REQUIREMENTS IN CASE OF LOSS: In the event of a fire loss, the policy does not permit the insured to abandon his property. He must use every possible precaution to protect the undamaged property against further

loss. The insured must comply with the following conditions:
- (a) Give immediate written loss to the company.
- (b) Safeguard the insured premises from further injury.
- (c) Immediately separate the damaged from the undamaged property and place it in good order.
- (d) Submit an itemized inventory, showing in detail quantities, costs, actual cash value and amount of loss claimed.
- (e) Submit a proof of loss, generally within 60 days, (unless written permission by the company extends this period).
- (f) Contents of the Proof of Loss
    - (a) Cause and time of fire.
    - (b) Nature of the insured's interest in the property damaged.
    - (c) Any other fire insurance covering same property.
    - (d) Outstanding liens held by third persons against the property covered.
    - (e) Produce on demand, as often as the company may reasonably request, bills and vouchers.
    - (f) Permit an inspection of the premises by the representatives of the insurance company.

PAYMENT OF LOSSES: In the event of a fire loss, the company sends an adjuster to determine the extent of the claim. Allowances are made for depreciation of property value at the time of loss. If the insured and the company are unable to come to terms, the parties are required to submit their disputed claim to appraisers selected by the insured and the company. These appraisers select a third party, a disinterested umpire, to decide in the event of a deadlock.

PAYMENT OF CLAIMS: Payment for the loss is required to be paid by the company, within 60 days after the Proof of Loss has been received, or by filing with the company an award which has been approved by the appraisers and the umpire.

If the insurance company, however, denies liability, and refuses to make any payment, the insured may sue for a recovery, provided that such action is started within one year from the date of the fire loss, and further provided, that he has complied with the requirements of the policy, e.g. written notice of loss, separation of damaged from undamaged property, etc.

Question: An insured suffers $1,000. fire damage to his premises. Is the insurance company obligated to pay this sum in cash, or may they offer to rebuild the damaged part?

Answer: Under the standard fire policy, the company has various options. The company may pay the insured the agreed or appraised loss value. It may also, if it so desires, repair, rebuild or replace the property destroyed or damaged, within a reasonable time, with materials of similar kind and quality. However, if the company intends to exercise its option to repair the property, it must so notify the insured in writing, within 30 days after receiving an acceptable Proof of Loss.

Question: Brown has suffered severe fire damage to his home. The building is completely gutted, and Brown is ordered by the local authorities to tear down the remains. Is Brown covered for his expenses to the housewrecker under his fire policy?

Answer: No. In order to be protected for such additional losses, the homeowner may request an endorsement providing for Demolition Damage Cost.

Question: John Smith owns a home valued at $20,000. The X Savings Bank has a mortgage lien on this house in the amount of $15,000. Under the terms of this mortgage, Smith is required to carry Fire Insurance in the sum of $15,000. for the benefit of the mortgagee. Thereafter, a fire occurs resulting in a $15,000. loss. What disposition must the mortgagee make of the proceeds of this insurance

Answer: The mortgagee is entitled to keep this money, and give the owner of the house, a satisfaction of the mortgage debt. The bank's investment has been protected. The owner should in all cases also carry sufficient additional insurance to protect his equity, that is, the amount of his cash payment plus any improvements made by him.

Co-Insurance Requirements

In order to equalize the cost of insurance and to penalize those who are under-insured, the standard fire policy requires a homeowner to carry at least 80 per cent of the total replacement value of the house if he wants to collect the full amount due him for any partial damage to the building.

There is a considerable amount of confusion on the part of the public concerning the application of this rule. Some people understand this clause to mean that the insurance company will only pay 80 per cent of any loss. Others feel that if there has been a total loss, the insurance company will pay only 80 per cent of the face amount of the policy. Actually, the co-insurance clause works this way. If a homeowner complies with the 80 per cent clause, (House worth $100,000.—80 per cent carried $80,000.) and lightning knocks down his chimney, tears off a part of the roof and otherwise does a total of $2,000. damage, the insured will collect $2,000. from the insurance company. If the house of the insured burns down to the ground, he will collect the face value of his policy. ($80,000.)

If he had carried only 40 per cent ($40,000.) the insured has only one-half of the required co-insurance amount, and therefore will collect only one-half of his loss, i.e., $1,000.

Policies may also be written by the insured calling for a 90 per cent or a 100 per cent clause. The following example should clarify the co-insurance requirements:

OWNER A

Actual cash value of property	$100,000.
80 per cent required	80,000.
Insurance actually carried	80,000.
Loss sustained	16,000.
Amount collectible	16,000.

In this case, the insured collects his full loss.

OWNER B
Actual cash value of property	$100,000.
80 per cent required	80,000.
Insurance actually carried	43,332.
Loss sustained	16,000.
Amount collectible	10,666.

In case of owner B, insured has carried only two-thirds of the required insurance ($100,000. required — $80,000. carried), therefore he will receive only two-thirds of his loss.

ADDITIONAL PROPERTY PERILS: The standard fire policy cannot meet all emergencies, and the insured generally requires a wider protection. To meet this need, a number of endorsements are available, for an additional premium, increasing the liability of the company for losses, caused other than by fire to the homeowner's property. This is called Extended Coverage, and the protection afforded under the various forms of Extended Coverage is very comprehensive. The endorsements available are the following:

(a) Windstorm and Hail (Shrubs, lawns, trees and plans and television aerials must be separately insured.)
(b) Explosion.
(c) Riots and Civil Disturbances.
(d) Smoke Damage.
(e) Falling Aircraft, Trucks or Passenger Cars damaging property.
(f) Vandalism and Malicious Mischief.

It is important to the owner to survey his needs and have them analyzed expertly so that adequate insurance is carried to meet the major hazards. The cost of the additional extended coverages is slight compared to the degree of protection offered.

LIABILITY INSURANCE: Minor accidents in or around a home may play havoc with family finances, unless the family is covered by Comprehensive Personal Liability Insurance. An individual, whether he owns or rents, is generally responsible for injury to anyone lawfully on his property. He is responsible for destruction caused by his servants; even for injury caused by his dog. In addition this policy covers all sports liability, e.g. fishing, golf, hunting accidents.

This is a heavy responsibility, but fortunately for the homeowner, it can be passed along to an insurance company, by taking out such a policy affording protection against these risks.

The cost of this policy is approximately $15. per year, (on a three year policy, one-half a year's premium is saved,) and the insurance company guarantees protection and will pay damages up to $10,000. if the policyholder is at fault.

Under such a policy, the company will also pay all expenses connected with any legal action involved, including lawyer's fees and medical expenses up to $250. for accidents to third persons, even if their injuries were not the fault of the policyholder.

The small premium required for such a policy will usually pay heavy dividends in security and financial stability.

THE NEW HOMEOWNER'S POLICY: Homeowners may now obtain a package deal under this new type of policy, which affords the following coverage:

(a) Fire and Lightning.
(b) Extended Coverages.
(c) Vandalism and Malicious Mischief.
(d) In addition, the Homeowner's Policy will reimburse an insured, for the necessary additional expense of living temporarily in a hotel or elsewhere, if the house is made untenantable by any of the above perils.
(e) This policy also includes Liability for personal injuries, including medical payments.
(f) Thefts from the insured's premises.
(g) Burglary of the premises.

The advantages of the Homeowner's Policy is the consolidation of risks in one policy, thereby eliminating overlapping coverages, and having one expiration date. If such protection is desired, insurance companies will give an insured credit for existing unexpired policies towards the issuance of the Homeowner's policy.

GLOSSARY

Abstract of Title A summary of the most important parts of all recorded instruments that affect the title to property, arranged in the order in which they were recorded.

Acre A measure of land equal to 160 square rods, or 4,840 square yards, or 43,560 square feet. (A plot of land approximately 200 feet wide and 200 feet deep is nearly an acre.)

Ad valorem According to value.

Adverse Possession The open and notorious possession of real property as a claim to title. Therefore, a method of acquiring title.

Agent One who acts for and has the authority to represent another who is known as a principal.

Air Rights Rights in real property to use the space above the surface of the real estate without precluding the use of its surface area for some other purpose.

Amenities, Amenity Return Pleasant satisfactions that are received through using rights in real property but that are not received in the form of money.

Amortization A gradual paying off of a debt by periodic installments.

Amortized Mortgage A mortgage in which repayment is made in accordance with a definite plan that requires the repayment of certain amounts at definite times so that all the debt is released by the end of the term.

Appraisal, Valuation An estimate of value. In real estate, an estimate of value of specific rights in a specific parcel of real estate as of a specific date for a specific purpose.

Appraisal Report A report, usually written, of the appraised value, together with the pertinent information regarding the property appraised and the evidence and analysis leading to the reported value estimate.

MAI (Member Appraisal Institute). A professional designation of an appraiser who is a member of the American Institute of Real Estate Appraisers, an association affiliated with the National Association of Real Estate Boards.

Appreciation A rise in value or price attributable to such factors as inflation, market conditions, improvements, location, etc.

Appurtenance Property that is an accessory to or incidental to other property to which it is annexed.

Assessment The valuation of a property for the purpose of levying a tax. The tax so levied.

> **Special Assessment** An assessment levied for a specific purpose such as providing streets, sewers, sidewalks, and the like. An assessment related to benefit derived by the taxed.

Assessor An official who has responsibility of determining assessed values for purposes of taxation.

Assumption of Mortgage The taking of title to property by a grantee, wherein he assumes liability for payment of an existing note or bond, secured by a mortgage against a property, and becomes personally liable for the payment of such mortgage debt.

Binder An agreement to cover the payment of purchase of real estate as evidence of good faith on the part of the purchaser.

Blanket Mortgage A mortgage that has two or more properties pledged or conveyed as security for a debt, usually for subdividing and improvement purposes.

Bond The evidence of a personal debt which is secured by a mortgage or other lien on real estate.

Building Codes Government regulations that specify minimum construction standards for the purpose of maintaining public health and safety.

Building Line A line fixed at a certain distance from the front and/or side of a lot beyond which no building can project.

Building Permit Authorization or permission by local government for the erection, alteration, or remodeling or improvements within its jurisdiction.

Certiori Proceedings A proceeding to review in a competent court the action of an inferior tribunal board or officer exercising judicial functions, widely used by property owners contesting real estate assessments on their property made by local assessors.

Chain of Title A history of conveyances and encumbrances affecting title from the time the original title was granted, or as far back as records are available.

Chattels Personal property; personality.

Chattel Mortgage A mortgage on personal property.

Closing Date The date upon which the buyer takes over the property, usually thirty to sixty days after the signing of the contract.

Closing Statement A listing of the debts and credits of the buyer and seller to a real estate transaction for the financial settlement of the transaction.

Cloudy Title See *Title,* cloudy title.

Commitment A pledge, or a promise, or an affirmation agreement. For a mortgage, a promise or statement by the lender of the terms and conditions under which he will lend.

Condemnation Taking private property for public use with fair compensation to the owner. Exercised right of "eminent domain."

Contract An agreement between two or more persons that is legally enforceable; a written evidence of such an agreement.

Conversion A change in the use of real estate without destruction of the improvements; a change in the use of real estate by altering improvements.

Conveyance The transfer of title of land from one to another. The means or medium by which title of real estate is tranferred.

Covenants Agreements written into deeds and other instruments promising performances, or nonperformances, of certain acts, or stipulating certain uses or nonuses of the property.

Credit Check Procedure taken by lending institutions in mortgage applications and other requests for financing whereby the personal and financial history of an applicant is obtained and evaluated to determine credibility and risk factors based upon past credit experience.

Deed An instrument conveying title to real property.

    Grant Deed A deed in which the seller warrants that he has not previously passed title.

    Quitclaim Deed An instrument transfering only such title as the seller may possess.

    Warranty Deed A deed in which the seller warrants that title is "good and merchantable."

Deed Restrictions Limitations placed upon the use of real property in the writing of a deed.

Deficiency Judgment A judgment for that part of a debt secured that was not liquidated by the proceeds from the sale of foreclosed property.

Depreciation Loss in value of real property brought about by age, physical deterioration, or financial or economic obsolescence.

Earnest Money Down payment made by a purchaser of real estate as evidence of good faith.

Easement The right to make limited use of real property owned by another; a right to use property without taking possession.

Eminent Domain The right of government to take private property for public use with just compensation.

Encroachment A building, part of a building, or obstruction which intrudes upon or invades property of another.

Encumbrance A claim against a property such as a debt secured by a mortgage.
Equity The interest or value which the owner has in real estate over and above the liens against it.
Erosion The wearing of ground surface.
Escheat The reversion of private property to the state.
Escrow A written agreement between two or more parties providing that certain instruments or properties be placed with a third party to be delivered to a designated person upon the fulfillment or performance of some act or condition.
Escrow Account A special financial account maintained by a lending institution, funded usually from a portion of the monthly mortgage payment of the borrower. The institution pays from this fund on behalf of the borrower obligations of taxes, insurance, etc., as they become due.
Estate The degree, quantity, nature, and extent of an interest in real property.
Eviction The taking possession of real property from one in possession.

Fidelity Bond A bond posted as security for the discharge of an obligation of personal services.
Foreclosure The legal steps required by law to be taken by the mortgagee after the default of a debt before the property can be proceeded against for payment of the debt.
> **Foreclosure by Sale** Foreclosure either under court action resulting in a decree of sale or under power of sale contained in a mortgage or trust deed.
> **Strict Foreclosure** Action by a court that, after determination that sufficient time has elapsed for a mortgagor to pay a mortgage past due, terminates all rights and interest of the mortgagor in the real property.

Grant A transfer of real property by written instrument as in a deed.
Grantee One who receives a transfer of real property by deed.
Grantor One who transfers real property by deed.
Grievance Day Period of time usually limited to one to three days designated by local taxing authorities to give property owners an opportunity to formally protest tax assessments. Notice of "grievance day" is usually well-publicized in advance. Property owners may contact office of taxing authority to obtain "grievance day" dates if normal source of publications not available or subscribed to.
Homestead (right of), homestead exemption The interest of the head of a family in his owned residence that is exempt from the claims of creditors.
Improved Value The difference between the income-producing ability of a property and the amount required to pay a return on the investment in the property.
Improvement That which is erected or constructed upon land to release the income-earning potential of the land; buildings or appurtenances on land.
Incorporeal Rights Nonpossessory rights in real estate.
Insured Mortgage A mortgage in which a party other than the borrower, in return for the payment or a premium, assures payment in the event of default by a mortgagor, e.g., FHA insured mortgages.
Judgment The acknowledgment or award of a claim through a court of law; an obligation or debt under a court decree; also, the decree.
Junior Mortgage A mortgage having claim ranking below that of another mortgage.
Lease A transfer of possession and the right to use property to a tenant for a stipulated period, during which the tenant pays rent to the owner; the contract containing the terms and conditions of such an agreement.
Legal Description, Land Description A means of identifying the exact boundaries of land by metes and bounds, by a plat, or by township and range survey system.

metes and bounds "Metes" refers to measures; "bounds" to direction. Metes and bounds are means of describing land by measurement and direction from a known point or marker on land.

plat A recorded map of land that identifies a parcel by a number or other designation in a subdivision.

township and range survey system A system of legal description of land with a township as the basic unit of measurement.

base line A parallel that serves as a reference for other parallels.

meridians North-south lines of survey 6 miles apart.

parallel East-west lines of survey 6 miles apart.

range A north-south row of townships; the 6-mile strip of land between meridians.

section A 1-mile square in a township.

tier An east-west row of townships; the 6-mile strip of land between parallels.

township A 6-mile square of land bounded by parallels and meridians, and composed of 36 sections.

Listing An agreement or contract providing that the agent shall receive a commission if the property is sold as a result of the efforts of that agent or any other agent, but not as a result of the efforts of the principal; the contract further provides that the agent will receive a commission if he secures a buyer under the terms of the contract.

Mortgage The pledge of real property to secure a debt; the conveyance of real property as security for a debt; the instrument that is evidence of the pledge or conveyance.

Mortgagee A party who lends money and takes a mortgage to secure the payment thereof.

Mortgagor A person who borrows money and gives a mortgage on his property as security for the payment of the debt.

Multiple Listing An arrangement among a group of real estate brokers whereby each broker presents his listing of property for sale to the attention of the others with a prearranged agreement pertaining to the sharing of commissions. If properly administered this system affords purchaser in dealing with one broker the exposure of all property available within a certain area.

Perpetuity Without limitation of time, perpetual.

Personal Property The exclusive right to exercise control over personality; all property objects other than real estate.

Personality All property other than realty; chattels.

Prepayment Clause A clause in a mortgage which gives a mortgagor the privilege of paying the mortgage indebtedness before it becomes due.

Principal One who has another act for him; one who is represented by an agent. Also, the amount of a debt.

Probate The proof or act of proving at a court that a last will and testament is actually the last will and testament of a deceased person.

Property The exclusive right to exercise control over economic good. See **Real Property; Personal Property**.

Property Taxes Taxes levied and collected from owners of real property administered by one or a combination of taxing authorities. Amounts and methods of taxation vary from one particular locale to another.

Purchase Money Mortgage A mortgage given by someone purchasing real property in part payment of the purchase price of real estate.

Real Estate In a physical sense, land with or without buildings or improvements; in a legal sense, the rights in such physical objects.

Real Estate Broker An agent who negotiates the sale of real property or real property services for a commission that is contingent on success.

Real Estate Syndicate A partnership organized for participation in a real estate venture. Partners may be limited or unlimited in their liability.

Real Property The exclusive right to exercise control over real estate; a parcel of real estate.

Realtor A broker who is a member of a local real estate board that is affiliated with the National Association of Real Estate Boards.

Realty The property objects of land and all things permanently attached to it.

Recording Acts, Registry Laws Laws providing for the recording of instruments affecting title as a matter of public record and that preserve such evidence and give notice of their existence and content; laws providing that the recording of an instrument informs all who deal in real property of the transaction and that unless the instrument is recorded, a prospective purchaser without actual notice of its existence is protected against it.

Redemption The regaining of title to real property after a foreclosure sale.

Registrar of Deeds, Recorder Officer in charge of a land records office.

Remainder The right of a person to interests that mature at the end of another estate; a classification of estates by time of enjoyment.

Rent Controls The legal provision for a maximum rental payment for the use of real property.

Reversion The residue of an estate left with the grantor that entitles him to possession after the end of another estate; a classification of estates by time of enjoyment.

Situs Location.

Specific Performance, Specifically Enforceable The requirement that a party must perform as agreed under a contract in contrast to compensation or damages in lieu of performance; the arrangement whereby courts may force either party to a real estate contract to carry out an agreement exactly.

Statute of Frauds Legislation providing that all agreements affecting title to real estate must be in writing to be enforceable.

Straight-term Mortgage A mortgage in which repayment of principal is in one lump sum at maturity.

Survey A measurement of land to determine boundaries or points of location on land; the process of determining, or the map that shows, the exact dimension and location of a site and possibly such things as levels of the land by contour lines, boundaries and their relationship to natural formations, and the location of streets, sewers, water, and gas and electric lines.

Tax Lien A claim against property arising out of nonpayment of taxes; the claim may be sold by the taxing authority.

Taxing District The geographical area over which a taxing authority levies taxes.

Title Proof or evidence of ownership or ownership rights.

> **abstract of title, abstract** A historical summary of the conveyances, transfers, and other facts relied on as evidence of title; a summary of the documents having a bearing on the history of the title to a property.
>
> **cloudy title** A title that would be impaired if an outstanding claim proved to be valid.
>
> **defective title** A title that would be impaired if an outstanding claim proved to be valid and where such a claim could be shown to be valid.
>
> **opinion of title** The statement, usually of an attorney, as to whether he believes a title to be clear or defective.
>
> **search of title** A study of the history of the title to a property.
>
> **tax title** The title to real property acquired through a forced sale for taxes; an interest in real property that will become ownership if the defaulting taxpayers does not redeem the property.
>
> **title by descent** Title acquired by the laws of succession; title acquired by an heir in the absence of a will.
>
> **title by devise** Title received through a will.

Title Insurance Insurance that a title is clear or clear except for defects noted; a policy of insurance that indemnifies the insured for loss occasioned by unknown defects of title.

Torrens System A system of land title registration in which the state guarantees title.

Trust Deed An instrument that is evidence of the pledge of real property as security for a debt where the title to the real property is held by a third party in trust while the debtor repays the debt to the lender; the debtor is known as the **trustor**; the lender is known as the **beneficiary**, the third party is known as the **trustee**.

Usury Charging more than the legal rate of interest for the use of money.

Vendee The seller of real estate, usually referred to as the party of the first part in an agreement of sale.

Warranty Deed One that contains a covenant that the grantor will protect the grantee against any claimant.

Zoning Ordinance Exercise of police power of a municipality in regulating and controlling the character and use of property.

INDEX

Accretion, 11
Adverse Possession, 7 ff.

Brokers
 acting for both parties, 83 ff.
 authority of, 86
 commissions, 81-82
 commissions rules, 89
 conflicting claims, 82
 deal failing due to fault of principal, 87
 duty of seller to broker, 87
 duties to seller, 87
 exclusives, 84 ff.
 opinions & representations, 92
 purchaser's agreement, 88
 rules of conduct, 91
 salesmen, as, 93
 secret profits, 88
 volunteers, 82

Contracts for Purchasing & Buying
 buyers & sellers check list, 79
 crops, 48-49
 date, 44
 description of, 45
 final closing preparations, 80
 importance of, 43
 meaning of, 44 ff.
 parties, 44
 personal property, 47-48

Deed
 bargain & sales, 24-25
 covenant & warranty, 21 ff.
 defined, 77
 execution & acknowledgment, 19
 quitclaim 26-27
 referee's, 29-31
 revenue stamps, 20

Eminent Domain, 2-3
Estate for Years, 13

Fee Simple, 12
Foreclosure, 9-11 (see also, Leases, Mortgages)
Future Estates, 13-14

Incumbrances & Defects of Title
 apportionment, 60
 form of deed, 61-62
 general, 49
 inability to perform, 65
 leases & tenancies, 54-55
 marketable titles & insurable titles, 55-56
 modification or changes, 65
 mortgages, 50-52 (see also, Mortgages)
 naming of broker, 64
 permission to purchaser to enter premises, 66-67
 possession, 67
 purchaser's liens, 62-63
 purchase money mortgages, 68
 risk of loss until closing, 58-60
 time and place of closing title, 63-64
 violations, 53

Insuring
  building property coverage, 105
  claims payment, 107-108
  co-insurance requirements, 109
  fire insurance, 104
  household contents coverage, 105
  obligation of company, 106
  payment of losses, 107

Joint Ownership, 14

Landlord & Tenant Relationship (see, Leases)
Leases
  assignment of, 102
  constructive eviction, 102
  execution & delivery of, 98
  foreclosure of mortgage, 102
  landlord liability, 101
  negotiation of, 98 ff.
  possession before title, 96 ff.
  premises, 99
  rent, 100
  rent control limitations, 95
  security deposit, 103
  term of, 100
  valid, 95

Mortgages
  in general, 36
  financing of, 34-36
  foreclosure (lease), 35
  forms, 37 ff.

Neighborhood Restrictions, 31 ff.

Real Estate
  defined, 4-5
  ownership of, 5
Recording, 15-16
Revenue Stamps, 20

Taxes & Assessments, 33-34
Tenants of Entirety, 15 ff.
Title
  deed of purchase, 6
  encumbrances, 73 ff.
  inheritance, 6-7
  Lis Pendens, 75 ff.
  search, 69 ff.

LEGAL ALMANAC SERIES CONVERSION TABLE
List of Original Titles and Authors

1. LAW OF MARRIAGE AND DIVORCE, R.V. MacKay
2. HOW TO MAKE A WILL SIMPLIFIED, P.J.T. Callahan
3. LAW OF ADOPTION, M.L. Leavy
4. LAW OF REAL ESTATE, P.J.T. Callahan
5. IMMIGRATION LAWS OF THE UNITED STATES, C.M. Crosswell
6. GUARDIANSHIP LAW, R.V. MacKay
7. LABOR LAW, C. Rachlin
8. HOW TO BECOME A CITIZEN OF THE U.S., Margaret E. Hall
9. SEX AND THE STATUTORY LAW, Part I, R.V. Sherwin
9a. SEX AND THE STATUTORY LAW, Part II, R.V. Sherwin
10. LAW OF DEBTOR AND CREDITOR, L.G. Greene
11. LANDLORD AND TENANT, F.H. Kuchler
12. LAW OF SUPPORT, F.H. Kuchler
13. CIVIL RIGHTS AND CIVIL LIBERTIES, E.S. Newman
14. LAW OF NOTARIES PUBLIC, L.G. Greene
15. LAW OF LIBEL AND SLANDER, E.C. Thomas
16. LIQUOR LAWS, B.M. Bernard
17. EDUCATION LAW, D.T. Marke
18. LAW OF MISSING PEOPLE, F. Fraenkel
19. STATE WORKMEN'S COMPENSATION, W.R. Dittmar
20. LAW OF MEDICINE, P.J.T. Callahan
21. HOW TO SECURE COPYRIGHT, R. Wincor
22. JUVENILE DELINQUENCY, F.B. Sussman
23. LAWS CONCERNING RELIGION, A. Burstein
24. ELECTION LAWS, B.M. Bernard
25. DRIVER'S MANUAL, T. Mattern & A.J. Mathes
26. STATE SOCIAL SECURITY LAWS, S.H. Asch
27. MANUAL OF CIVIL AVIATION LAW, T. Mattern & A.J. Mathes
28. HOW TO PROTECT AND PATENT YOUR INVENTION, I. Mandell
29. LAW FOR THE SMALL BUSINESSMAN, M.L. Leavy
30. INSANITY LAWS, W.R. Dittmar
31. HOW TO SERVE ON A JURY, P. Francis
32. CRIMES AND PENALTIES, T.B. Stuchiner
33. LAW OF INHERITANCE, E.M. Wypyski
34. HOW TO CHANGE YOUR NAME, L.G. Greene
35. LAW OF ACCIDENTS, W.M. Kunstler
36. LAW OF CONTRACTS, R. Wincor
37. LAW OF INSURANCE, I.M. Taylor
38. LAW OF PHILANTHROPY, E.S. Newman
39. LAW OF SELLING, J.A. Hoehlein
40. LAW OF PERSONAL LIBERTIES, R. Schwartzmann
41. LAW OF BUYING AND SELLING, B.R. White
42. PRACTICAL AND LEGAL MANUAL FOR THE INVESTOR, S.I. Kaufman
43. LAW FOR THE HOMEOWNER, REAL ESTATE OPERATOR, AND BROKER, L.M. Nussbaum
44. LAW FOR THE TOURIST, R.J. DeSeife
45. LAW FOR THE FAMILY MAN, L.F. Jessup
46. LEGAL STATUS OF YOUNG ADULTS, P.J.T. Callahan
47. LAW AND THE SPORTSMAN, R.M. Debevec
48. LAW OF RETIREMENT, L.F. Jessup
49. LAW FOR THE PET OWNER, D.S. Edgar
50. ESTATE PLANNING, P.J. Goldberg
51. TAX PLANNING, P.J. Goldberg
52. LEGAL PROTECTION FOR THE CONSUMER, S. Morganstern
53. LEGAL STATUS OF WOMEN, P. Francis
54. PRIVACY—ITS LEGAL PROTECTION, H. Gross
55. PROTECTION THROUGH THE LAW, P. Francis
56. LAW OF ART AND ANTIQUES, S. Hodes
57. LAW OF DEATH AND DISPOSAL OF THE DEAD, H.Y. Bernard
58. LAW DICTIONARY OF PRACTICAL DEFINITIONS, E.J. Bander
59. LAW OF ENGAGEMENT AND MARRIAGE, F.H. Kuchler
60. CONDEMNATION: YOUR RIGHTS WHEN GOVERNMENT ACQUIRES YOUR PROPERTY, G. Lawrence
61. CONFIDENTIAL AND OTHER PRIVILEGED COMMUNICATION, R.D. Weinberg
62. UNDERSTANDING THE UNIFORM COMMERCIAL CODE, D. Lloyd
63. WHEN AND HOW TO CHOOSE AN ATTORNEY, C.K. Wehringer
64. LAW OF SELF-DEFENSE, F.S. & J. Baum
65. ENVIRONMENT AND THE LAW, I.J. Sloan
66. LEGAL PROTECTION IN GARNISHMENT AND ATTACHMENT, S. Morganstern
67. HOW TO BE A WITNESS, K.Tierney
68. AUTOMOBILE LIABILITY AND THE CHANGING LAW, M.G. Woodroof
69. PENALTIES FOR MISCONDUCT ON THE JOB, A. Avins
70. LEGAL REGULATION OF CONSUMER CREDIT, S. Morganstern
71. RIGHT OF ACCESS TO INFORMATION FROM THE GOVERNMENT, S.D. Thurman
72. COOPERATIVES AND CONDOMINIUMS, P.E. Kehoe
73. RIGHTS OF CONVICTS, H.I. Handman
74. FINDING THE LAW-GUIDE TO LEGAL RESEARCH, D. Lloyd
75. LAWS GOVERNING BANKS AND THEIR CUSTOMERS, S. Mandell
76. HUMAN BODY AND THE LAW, C.L. Levy
77. HOW TO COPE WITH U.S. CUSTOMS, A.I. Demcy

LEGAL ALMANAC SERIES CONVERSION TABLE
List of Present Titles and Authors

1. LAW OF SEPARATION AND DIVORCE, 4th Ed., P.J.T. Callahan
2. HOW TO MAKE A WILL/HOW TO USE TRUSTS, 4th Ed., P.J.T. Callahan
3. LAW OF ADOPTION, 4th Ed., M.L. Leavy & R.D. Weinberg
4. REAL ESTATE LAW FOR HOMEOWNER AND BROKER, P.J.T. Callahan & L.M. Nussbaum
5. ELIGIBILITY FOR ENTRY TO THE U.S., 3rd Ed., R.D. Weinberg
6. LAW OF GUARDIANSHIPS, R.V.MacKay
7. LABOR LAW, 3rd Ed., D. Epp
8. HOW TO BECOME A CITIZEN OF THE U.S., L.F. Jessup
9. SEXUAL CONDUCT AND THE LAW, 2nd Ed., G. Mueller
10. LAW OF CREDIT, 2nd Ed., L.G. Greene
11. LANDLORD AND TENANT, Rev. Ed., L.F. Jessup
12. LAW OF SUPPORT, 2nd Ed., F.H. Kuchler
13. CIVIL LIBERTY AND CIVIL RIGHTS, 6th Ed., P.S. Newman
14. LAW OF NOTARIES PUBLIC, 2nd Ed., L.G. Greene
15. LAW OF LIBEL AND SLANDER, 3rd Ed., E.C. Thomas
16. LAWS GOVERNING AMUSEMENTS, R.M. Debevec
17. SCHOOLS AND THE LAW, 3rd Ed., E.E. Reutter
18. FAMILY PLANNING AND THE LAW, 2nd Ed., R.D. Weinberg
19. STATE WORKMEN'S COMPENSATION, W.R. Dittmar
20. MEDICARE, S. Goldberger
21. HOW TO SECURE COPYRIGHT, 2nd Ed., R. Wincor
22. LAW OF JUVENILE JUSTICE, S. Rubin
23. LAWS CONCERNING RELIGION, 2nd Ed., M.B. Burstein
24. ELECTION PROCESS, A. Reitman & R.B. Davidson
25. DRIVER'S MANUAL, Rev. Ed., T. Mattern & A.J. Mathes
26. PUBLIC OFFICIALS, H.Y. Bernard
27. MANUAL OF CIVIL AVIATION LAW, T. Mattern & A.J. Mathes
28. HOW TO PROTECT AND PATENT YOUR INVENTION, I. Mandell
29. LAW FOR THE BUSINESSMAN, B.D. Reams, Jr.
30. PSYCHIATRY, THE LAW, AND MENTAL HEALTH, S. Pearlstein
31. HOW TO SERVE ON A JURY, 2nd Ed., P. Francis
32. CRIMES AND PENALTIES, 2nd Ed., B.R. White
33. LAW OF INHERITANCE, 3rd Ed., E.M. Wypyski
34. CHANGE OF NAME AND LAW OF NAMES, 2nd Ed., E.J. Bander
35. LAW OF ACCIDENTS, W.M. Kunstler
36. LAW OF CONTRACTS, 2nd Ed., R. Wincor
37. LAW OF INSURANCE, 2nd Ed., E.M. Taylor
38. LAW OF PHILANTHROPY, E.S. Newman
39. ARBITRATION PRECEPTS AND PRINCIPLES, C.K. Wehringer
40. THE BILL OF RIGHTS AND THE POLICE, Rev. Ed., M. Zarr
41. LAW OF BUYING AND SELLING, 2nd Ed., B.R. White
42. THE INVESTOR'S LEGAL GUIDE, 2nd Ed., S.I. Kaufman
43. LEGAL STATUS OF LIVING TOGETHER, I.J. Sloan (LAW FOR HOMEOWNER, REAL ESTATE OPERATOR, AND BROKER, see no. 4)
44. LAW BOOKS FOR NON-LAW LIBRARIES AND LAYMEN, A BIBLIOGRAPHY, R.M. Mersky
45. NEW LIFE STYLE AND THE CHANGING LAW, 2nd Ed., L.F. Jessup
46. YOUTH AND THE LAW, 3rd Ed., I.J. Sloan
47. LAW AND THE SPORTSMAN, R.M. Debevec
48. LAW OF RETIREMENT, 2nd Ed., L.F. Jessup
49. LAW FOR THE PET OWNER, D.S. Edgar
50. INCOME AND ESTATE TAX PLANNING, I.J. Sloan
51. TAX PLANNING, see no. 50
52. LEGAL PROTECTION FOR THE CONSUMER, 2nd Ed., S. Morganstern
53. LEGAL STATUS OF WOMEN, 2nd Ed., P. Francis
54. PRIVACY—ITS LEGAL PROTECTION, 2nd Ed., H. Gross
55. PROTECTION THROUGH THE LAW, 2nd Ed., P. Francis
56. LAW OF ART AND ANTIQUES, S. Hodes
57. LAW OF DEATH AND DISPOSAL OF THE DEAD, 2nd Ed., H.Y. Bernard
58. DICTIONARY OF SELECTED LEGAL TERMS AND MAXIMS, 2nd Ed., E.J. Bander
59. LAW OF ENGAGEMENT AND MARRIAGE, 2nd Ed., F.H. Kuchler
60. CONDEMNATION: YOUR RIGHTS WHEN GOVERNMENT ACQUIRES YOUR PROPERTY, G. Lawrence
61. CONFIDENTIAL AND OTHER PRIVILEGED COMMUNICATION, R.D. Weinberg
62. UNDERSTANDING THE UNIFORM COMMERCIAL CODE, D. Lloyd
63. WHEN AND HOW TO CHOOSE AN ATTORNEY, 2nd Ed., C.K. Wehringer
64. LAW OF SELF-DEFENSE, F.S. & J. Baum
65. ENVIRONMENT AND THE LAW, 2nd Ed., I.J. Sloan
66. LEGAL PROTECTION IN GARNISHMENT AND ATTACHMENT, S. Morganstern
67. HOW TO BE A WITNESS, K. Tierney
68. AUTOMOBILE LIABILITY AND THE CHANGING LAW, M.G. Woodroof
69. PENALTIES FOR MISCONDUCT ON THE JOB, A. Avins
70. LEGAL REGULATION OF CONSUMER CREDIT, S. Morganstern
71. RIGHT OF ACCESS TO INFORMATION FROM THE GOVERNMENT, S.D. Thurman
72. COOPERATIVES AND CONDOMINIUMS, P.E. Kehoe
73. RIGHTS OF CONVICTS, H.I. Handman
74. FINDING THE LAW-GUIDE TO LEGAL RESEARCH, D. Lloyd
75. LAWS GOVERNING BANKS AND THEIR CUSTOMERS, S. Mandell
76. HUMAN BODY AND THE LAW, C.L. Levy
77. HOW TO COPE WITH U.S. CUSTOMS, A.I. Demcy